THE
Treasure
IS WITHIN

JANE-LOUISE KELLY

BALBOA
PRESS
A DIVISION OF HAY HOUSE

Balboa Press books may be ordered through booksellers or by contacting:

Balboa Press
A Division of Hay House
1663 Liberty Drive
Bloomington, IN 47403
www.balboapress.com
1 (877) 407-4847

Because of the dynamic nature of the Internet, any web addresses or links contained in this book may have changed since publication and may no longer be valid. The views expressed in this work are solely those of the author and do not necessarily reflect the views of the publisher, and the publisher hereby disclaims any responsibility for them.

The author of this book does not dispense medical advice or prescribe the use of any technique as a form of treatment for physical, emotional, or medical problems without the advice of a physician, either directly or indirectly. The intent of the author is only to offer information of a general nature to help you in your quest for emotional and spiritual well-being. In the event you use any of the information in this book for yourself, which is your constitutional right, the author and the publisher assume no responsibility for your actions.

Any people depicted in stock imagery provided by Thinkstock are models, and such images are being used for illustrative purposes only.
Certain stock imagery © Thinkstock.

Print information available on the last page.

ISBN: 978-1-5043-6730-1 (sc)
ISBN: 978-1-5043-6731-8 (hc)
ISBN: 978-1-5043-6772-1 (e)

Library of Congress Control Number: 2016916493

Balboa Press rev. date: 11/05/2016

With stillness of being comes peace of heart.
With peace of heart comes the sharing of love.
Love cultivates peace and joy
And the whole world rejoices.

Jane-Louise Kelly

Introduction

A CHARMED LIFE

I was once told by a friend that I lived a 'charmed' life. It was not, however, until my life's calm was deeply perturbed that I realized what real charm is.

I believe now that it is the capacity to know, profoundly, that all is well when reality would suggest otherwise.

This was the life lesson I was about to be introduced to, and the writings of this book were a lifeline to me when I feared I would lose all faith in life and in myself.

And I did, for a while.

I had been writing to Spirit in written form for guidance, reassurance and wisdom for my personal journey for many years. I had begun, in my early twenties, by attempting to connect with my inner child through the guidance of a book that I had picked up in a bookshop I loved to pop into on my way back home from my first proper job in Brussels, Belgium. I started by using my non-dominant hand to initiate communication with my inner child. At the beginning the communication looked like scribbles and childish drawings that were, nevertheless, opening me to a new world within. With time I was able to type out, on the keyboard of my computer, questions and receive answers that seemed to be coming from somewhere very peaceful, loving and all-knowing, beyond my mind. I started to ask questions to which I received answers that helped me gain a new perspective on my life. Eventually what I was receiving became so allegoric and general in nature that I decided to ask a question every day for a whole year with the intention of eventually sharing the answers in one form or another. That journey went beyond a year and continues still now as I approach my forty-seventh birthday.

It was only after the completion of part one of these writings that I asked who I was speaking to.

> Speaking to you now is your Higher Office. Within this Higher Office is your Soul Self presiding with many other beings of advanced light who have invested in you, their hopes and desires. We are an agglomeration of hopes and desires that were spoken before you came into being as the Jane-Louise that you now are.

This term 'Higher Office' was not new to me. I had been asked in prior channels to call them my Higher Office as a playful take on the word higher, encouraging me to 'hire' their services whenever I so choose. However, it was made clear that this relationship is not unique to me as we all have a Higher Office to call on.

> Behind each human 'being' is this same community of hopes and desires spoken before your very existence. And so we are you and you are us, for we were birthed with the same intention of Spirit. And so, when you call on us, you open yourself to many levels of knowing that are perfectly attuned

to the life that you desire to live for they are contained in the initial spoken intention that we all subscribed to. And so every answer that you search is contained within this portal to yourself, the community of 'All That You Are', and the desires and dreams that you have held and upheld for aeons of time.

We desire for you to know that our attention in your regard is never-ending and complete. We are literally at your every beck and call, urging you in the direction of your greatest desires. When there is resistance we find it difficult to be fully efficient but when you let go in trust that all is working out for the best then indeed it does.

We would ask you to trust your Self, which is the agglomeration of all your hopes, desires and dreams, which is in fact us, to lead you in the direction of your complete fulfilment. All is deeply well and when we work together nothing is too big or small for us to complete. We are the God that you have been looking for, the God of your dreams and desires and your fulfilment.

Peace to you. You are loved deeply, truly and completely and all is very well indeed.

I`M DONE!

I consider it naive now but I really wanted to believe, after completing the first part of this book, that I had been given the secret to life and that I was somehow 'done'. I imagined that I just had to live according to the wisdom contained in these writings and that all would be well.

3

Little did I know that this book was only a manual for the real learning, which is life itself and the complete embracing of it, come what may.

Come what may, did.

Six months after completing part one of this book, and what I believed would be this book in entirety, the rug was literally pulled from underneath my family's feet.

In August 2009, three weeks before his ninth birthday, our youngest son Toby was diagnosed with a highly malignant brain tumour. When cancer came to our door I felt abandoned by life, by my faith, by my Higher Office, by God. Who would ever have thought that our little one, the chubby huggable happy little boy we adored, would get cancer? I had breastfed him for two years, not vaccinated him until we moved from the Emirates, and only then because we were moving to Cameroon, West Africa. I had fed him as much organic food as I could find. He loved fruit and his favourite vegetable was raw broccoli. How come he was the one to get cancer? Why? What in heaven or hell's name was this? His name means 'the goodness of God'. What was in any way good about any of this? Honestly, I told my Higher Office to take a hike, a big one, and to take their sweet words with them! I was done!

And, of course, I *was* done. I was done with a mindset that was about to be rigorously and meticulously deconstructed. The real journey was only beginning and this is the part of the journey that I wish to share.

THE TASK IS TO BRING HEAVEN TO EARTH

For a long time I could not read the words in this book or even write again. I was just too sad and hurt by life. However these words had already penetrated my soul and their tiny seedlings of love were germinating in my darkness, urging me to find my way forward.

Heaven speaks to us in so many ways but we are the ones doing the journey here. We are the ones tasked, no matter how hard that may be, with translating that heavenly language into every aspect of our lives here on Earth, and that is what the journey I am about to relate really challenged me, and continues to challenge me, in every way to do.

THE BEGINNING

When my son was diagnosed with brain cancer I felt a mixture of absolute determination to help him in every way, coupled with such bewilderment, overwhelm and simple pain, as I watched him battle through his treatment.

Initially I would vacillate between telling my Higher Office to leave me alone and then call out to them for help. I would say bitterly, "It's all very well for you to sit in your heavenly place offering advice. Get your holy butts down here and start walking your talk and let's see how you do. This is too much!" I would feel disrespectful after such an outburst knowing in fact that they would gladly walk it for me, and then I would feel resigned, realizing painfully that I was the one with the butt here and that I just had to get on with it.

On so many levels this diagnosis and its treatment were unacceptable to me. I had always favoured natural methods to healing. We avoided doctors and went to healers and alternative practitioners when necessary. I was a Reiki practitioner and a Signature Cell Healer® and was reading every spiritual book going.

I had read all of the Ringing Cedar Series' books and, as a result, had bought the plot of land behind us where my husband and boys had built a tree house, and we were about to plant an edible forest garden so that we could eat what we grew. I was eating mainly a raw plant based diet and was a teacher and practitioner of yoga.

A linguist by training, I had had interesting jobs after my degree in French and German. I worked as a project coordinator in Brussels on European funded programmes, taught English in schools in Germany and the Emirates, and had the pure joy of working for half a year with a French speaking architect on the building site of a new palace in Abu Dhabi. However when we finally returned, after twelve years away, to live in my home country of Northern Ireland, I wanted to find a job that would allow me to work when our boys were at school. I needed a job that corresponded to my ever increasing interest in and hunger for all things spiritual. I trained as a yoga teacher, specializing in yoga for special needs children. I set up an organization called Yogabuddies and taught yoga to children and special needs children, and yoga teachers who wished to learn the methods I was using.

I was working hard at getting it all right; mum, wife, yoga teacher, energy healing worker, secret channeler, gardener, head of a budding organization, and active 'enlightenment' seeker!

WE WILL DO THIS TOGETHER

There is no preparation for a cancer diagnosis especially when it concerns your child. There is no parenting manual. No one tells you how to navigate this new territory. However, you feel that everyone around you is quietly desperate for you to cope and succeed, for the alternative is unthinkable.

I am so deeply grateful to those very courageous mothers and fathers with whom I walked this path and those wise souls who knew what to say to me when I most needed it. They were the ones that understood the pain and had no desire to cure me, fix me, judge me or change me but would see through my suffering and simply remind me of my inner strength, confident that I had the answer to my every problem or need. They offered compassion rather than sympathy. They would support me with such kindness and gentleness, sometimes without words at all. It was as if they stepped over this invisible boundary that would allow them to nurture my soul. Often these were people that seemed to know the world that I had been catapulted into. When I was with them I would feel my heart open and my breath expand. I would feel like myself, just not another mother and patient. Their very presence was like medicine to the soul and in this presence I would feel myself being transported somewhere safe.

There are angels everywhere in the form of individuals, who despite restrictions from systems or protocols, always find a way to support those they are looking after. I think goodness arises from individual offerings daily; people working quietly and selflessly for the common good, and I am so very deeply grateful to each of these individuals. It is very difficult to hold the space for someone else's pain but those that do it with compassion are very special people indeed.

One particular friend always had a beautiful way of reminding me that I was Toby's mum and that I knew exactly what to do. It sounded so obvious when she said it. I knew I knew somewhere deep in my soul; this was my child, born to me and through me. I wanted to whisk him away, take him to a shaman somewhere in the deep Amazonian forest who would magically cure him and make it all alright, and I did search for all alternative routes to healing. In a moment of desperation at the treatment that lay ahead I suggested to our neurosurgeon that I take Toby to a shaman but he just gently asked me to trust him to be the first to help Toby.

It took eight months of visits to many professionals to diagnose our son. From the moment of Toby's diagnosis and his immediate transport by ambulance to the children's hospital our families rallied around us. My husband, my parents, our oldest son, who was eleven at the time, my brother and my sister-in-law spent hours a day together during the first few days before the initial operation playing board games in the large spacious hallway of the children's hospital in Belfast so that we could all be together. Thanks to the steroids Toby was not enduring his habitual headaches and nausea and was in great form and enjoying everyone's company.

On the morning of the operation to remove his tumour, four days after his admittance to hospital, I had my first experience of an operating theatre where I watched Toby being put to sleep. I could feel the intensity of focus of the operating team around me and the nurse close to my side, ready to whisk me away when Toby went under. I left my precious child there in that operating theatre hoping that he had heard my last `I love you`. I thought my heart would break.

I remember being concerned that nine or ten hours in an operating theatre would be too much for the neurosurgeon and being even more shocked when he reassured me that he got breaks and had a very comfortable chair with arm rests. "And what happens to Toby while you`re having a break?" I tried to ask without sounding panicked. Of course Toby was being monitored constantly by a large and competent team, overseen by an anaesthetist, who happened to be from Australia.

Our neurosurgeon said firmly that he did not want us hanging around the hospital during the operation; the wait would be long and all the more painful for us if we stayed there. He wanted us to go out and get some fresh air. Noah, our oldest child, went to my parents` home and Ghislain, my husband, and I headed back to our hometown, Holywood, for a cup of tea. It was very strange just to be the two of us outside the hospital environment where we had been around the clock for the previous four days surrounded by family. We did not feel like going home to an empty house so we decided to treat ourselves to a cup of tea in our home town, and by chance met a dear friend who came to sit with us.

We sat together in the cafe as the sun shone through the window. As I placed the teacup to my mouth I was, without warning, overcome with emotion. In my mind`s eye I saw Toby very clearly. I saw him hover above his body in the operating theatre and I knew instinctively that the operation had begun in earnest. Toby was breathing heavily, every breath laden with worry and overwhelm. He was saying very clearly in a panicked voice, "I didn`t realize it was going to be this difficult. I didn`t realize it was going to be like this. This is too difficult. This is too much".

I felt his emotion wave through me as I promised him, through my own stifled sobs, that he would not do one part of the journey alone but that I would be with him the whole way. We would do it together.

My sister, Toby's godmother, was on a flight from Sydney to Melbourne, Australia, at the same time, and told me later that she experienced Toby's presence as if he was up in the clouds, away from the experience in the operating theatre. It was as if he wanted to distance himself from the intensity of the physical experience. She felt that he was scared and also repeated to him, "Everything's going to be ok Toby, don't worry!"

As I repeatedly reassured Toby that he would not have to do this alone, his breathing began to calm down and I felt him appeased, quietened and resolute. I opened my eyes to see my beautiful husband and dear friend looking at me.

Rather than feel distraught from this experience with Toby I felt strangely encouraged and a lightness of being came over me for the rest of that afternoon. Ghislain and I went shopping of all things, buying new pyjamas and a dressing gown for Toby as well as a vibrant pretty magenta top for me. It felt good to be just the two of us, and we knew this was precious time together before the challenges that lay ahead.

Back at the hospital that evening we approached the door of the intensive care unit ready to see Toby. The anaesthetist greeted us outside the door and commented immediately on my very colourful magenta top. It was as if, momentarily, we were all in a different place in time. Remembering all too quickly why we were there the anaesthetist explained with great care that the operation had gone to plan and that Toby was coming around slowly. Toby had survived and the entirety of his tumour had been removed.

I approached Toby's bed, wincing at the colour of blood in his blond hair, and the sight of his swollen lips and skin. He had a long incision along the middle of the back of his head. He opened his eyes slowly and looking at my new magenta top he said with amusement in his eyes, "You look much too posh to be in here", and with that closed his eyes and was not able to say another word for two weeks.

Before surgery the neurosurgeon had hoped Toby's tumour was benign but the operation itself and a biopsy confirmed several days later that it was the worst on the list that we had been presented with prior to surgery. It was a medulloblastoma; a grade IV malignant tumour growing in the cerebellum. The good news was that a lumbar puncture revealed no spread along the spinal column.

A REBIRTH

One evening following this initial operation it was my turn to stay with Toby during the night at the hospital. Ghislain and I did an alternative shift so that we would get one night's sleep out of two at home in a bed and in the quiet. Toby had gone to sleep and I was alone with him. We had pulled closed the pink curtains around his bed to get a little privacy and I was listening to music to drown out the busyness and noise of the ward. I was allowing myself to relax and cry peacefully at the sweet beauty of the music, and suddenly Toby appeared directly in front of me so much larger than life. His head was hitting the ceiling of the ward and he looked down on me with fullness and radiance. It was an extraordinary experience and in that moment I felt like he was being reborn to me. I sobbed with joy and relief.

This was such a life-affirming moment among the dreary reality of Toby's day to day life which was so difficult. He had to learn to walk, talk and eat again. His aim was to be able to walk up and down the stairs unaided, in time to leave the hospital for his ninth birthday in three weeks. We tried to be funny and make light of the challenges and developed a wry sense of humour to match Toby's.

NEVER GIVE UP

Despite his courage I knew Toby had felt like giving up. He was still feeling groggier than the nurses considered normal days after this initial nine hour operation to remove the plum size tumour on his cerebellum. As it transpired later, he was suffering from an abnormal accumulation of cerebrospinal fluid in the brain, known as hydrocephalus, which was causing increased intracranial pressure and making his recovery particularly difficult.

Toby's neurosurgeon arrived to the ward, with a little student posse, to check on his progress. I remember the neurosurgeon being particularly concerned with Toby, "Toby, I know you want to win. Are you a winner or a loser?" Nobody expected Toby to answer "A loser..." There was a sharp intake of breath and the posse left.

I had been primed by a very caring doctor in the intensive care unit, following Toby's first operation, to know that Toby would hit rock bottom before making any recovery. So I was cautioned not to panic when things looked dire as it would probably be an indication of the turning point. How low was low though?

As it happened, our favourite ward cleaner had been in the ward while the neurosurgeon and his student posse visited and had obviously heard much of the goings-on. When the posse left and the ward was quiet she started to clean around and under Toby's bed. "All these men are alike," she started, "just lying in their beds, feeling sorry for themselves while us poor women have to keep working, cleaning around them, keeping everything spotless. Feeling sorry for themselves, that's all they do. No work, just lying there; doing nothing!" On and on she went until Toby started to smile. He got her point and in it was the turning point. This very wonderful woman had accomplished what no one else had. A mop in hand and a heart full of compassion, humility and the type of dry humour Toby loved, she got my child around one of the hardest corners of his life.

Two years into Toby's treatment and rehabilitation he was asked an interesting question by the clinical psychologist. After weeks of tests to see what damage had been wreaked by the cancer treatment on Toby's mental and cognitive capacities I asked our clinical psychologist to address the emotional trauma Toby may have experienced. It occurred to me that we had not given as much professional attention to the emotional upheaval of the experience itself as we had to the necessary physical rehabilitation which, at that time, involved visits to nine professionals not including the complementary therapists that were assisting us.

Chemotherapy and radiotherapy destroy not only cancer cells but other perfectly functioning cells on their way. Because of the tumour itself, the operation to remove it and the treatment to mop up any residual cancer Toby has sustained damage to his eyesight, hearing, balance, digestion, hair, energy levels and endocrine system. These are disabilities that he lives with and that require monitoring, supervision and intervention on an ongoing basis. His tally of operations stands at eleven. And yet you need to look very closely at Toby to know that he lives with such difficulties. And to know him is to realize that these difficulties do not define him.

The clinical psychologist had a very interesting question, in itself empowering and healing. He asked Toby what he would say to children who have just received the same diagnosis and are about to go through a similar experience. They had this discussion without me being present and took great pleasure in presenting their conclusions. The clinical psychologist announced that Toby said, "They should eat their vegetables!" I laughed out loud as soon as they told me this as Toby and I have daily discussions about his intake of fruit and vegetables. Toby smiled, "That was just random, mum!" And so the psychologist continued to the heart of the matter. He told me that Toby said, "Never give up, even if you feel like it. Take the advice you get from those around you and just keep going".

Noah, Toby's older brother, had taken me aside in the early days of Toby's diagnosis. He was only eleven at the time but, looking at me very intently, told me that it was really time now for me to put all that 'positive thinking talk I do' into action!

I was always positive in front of Toby. I knew that he needed us to be confident and wholly convinced of his ability to move through every challenge courageously and with good humour, and he has and continues to do so. He was always courageous for his treatments, even when it scared him, and he learned to breathe deeply so that he could relax himself completely and stay stock-still during the MRI scans and radiotherapy treatment. When people asked him how he was, no matter how he was feeling, he would smile and say, "Very good thank you". I love spending time with him. He is serene, stoic and very wise. When asked to write a prayer for him by a friend, whose church group was prepared to pray for him, I wrote, without hesitation, "May God be praised for blessing us all with the love that is Toby". I didn't want to ask for healing. I simply wanted to be grateful for the gift that Toby is.

AN ABYSS OF DESPAIR

It was the torment in my own mind that was the real enemy. I felt like I had failed Toby.

I had been a vocal proponent of the 'Law of Attraction', talking about it in my workshops. Now I was really wondering how I or my family could have attracted this into our life. So when the question was asked directly of me, "Do you really think you created this Jane-Louise?" I met face to face with despair because, yes, somewhere I believed I had.

I found myself alone three weeks after Toby's initial operation. Noah was already asleep and Ghislain was out with his sister and nephew who were over from Belgium for Toby's ninth birthday celebration. I felt, for the first time in my life, a darkness of despair arise, and I reached to text my family for support. For some reason my texts would not go through, and I knew this was a bridge I needed to cross alone.

I saw the endlessness of despair as plainly as I see this computer screen before me. I was struck by crippling self-judgement, believing that somehow I had created this unbearable reality; that I had brought this on us, either by not being a good enough mother or as a form of punishment for misdoings whether in this life or a past life or a combination of all of the above. Either way I was ready to punish myself for it.

I felt the curtain fall as I stood literally and physically in my mind's eye at the edge of what looked like an eternally dark and endless abyss. I saw myself standing on a very small orange-coloured sandy outcrop of a cliff edge. Everything behind me was a vast, empty and endless desert of a dusty and rusty hue and beyond the cliff edge was an eternal abyss of darkness that was as wide as it was deep. The temptation to crumble before its vastness was great but thankfully in the same moment I remembered the life-saving advice that an intuitive had given me years before about embracing my emotions rather than resisting them and, in that initial meeting with despair, I consciously and physically embraced the abyss that lay all around and before me. In between body wrenching sobs I breathed it consciously into my being right down into my fingers and toes until I fell asleep.

Many times over the year of Toby's chemotherapy treatment I would be called to do this regularly. I had stopped crying because I was afraid if I started I would not be able to stop. On many occasions, especially towards the end of the eight six weekly treatments when the chemotherapy was beginning to accumulate in Toby's body, I would awake and not feel capable of facing a day of watching my son sick and unable to eat, unsure of whether he was actually getting better or slowly being reinvaded by this cancer. I would again consciously embrace the despair and then give myself over to my angels, asking them to look after me. Inevitably I would fall asleep imagining myself being taken somewhere sweet and special where I would be nurtured. I would sleep for no more than another ten to twenty minutes but would awaken stronger and lighter for the day ahead.

It was only in the rereading of this book that I realized the full significance of the story of 'The unbridled horse' which I received six months *before* Toby's diagnosis. It reads:

> You did not fall into the abyss. You fell into the wings of change and the sea of motion. You were not crushed by the powerful waves nor did you fall onto the jagged rocks. No, you sprouted wings.

It would take me quite a while before I would have any sense of the freedom of those wings.

PAIN AND BLISS

At Christmas of 2009 we were four months post diagnosis, and the initial operation, to remove the tumour. These four months had already consisted of five additional operations: one to put in `Mr. Wiggly` which is a catheter that sat in Toby's chest for the entirety of his treatment through which he gave blood and received his chemotherapy, two more unexpected operations to insert a shunt following the first week of radiotherapy, and another two to replace the first shunt several weeks after the completion of the six week radiotherapy treatment.

Toby had already had difficulty with an over-accumulation of cerebrospinal fluid in the brain following the initial operation to remove his tumour. During the difficult weeks post-op his situation had eventually stabilized however the swelling and inflammation, from the first week of radiotherapy treatment to Toby's head and spine, tipped the balance unfavourably again and we had to rush him to hospital with violent vomiting and headaches. He required an operation to insert a temporary drain into his brain and three days later another operation, his fourth in less than two months, to insert a permanent shunt which would drain away the excess cerebral spinal fluid that was accumulating within his skull.

Within less than a week he was out of hospital but the radiotherapy was so crucial in the cancer treatment protocol for his tumour that he was required to continue immediately with a six day, rather than a five day a week, radiotherapy programme over the remaining five weeks of treatment. We actually have fond memories of this treatment phase because Toby's godmother, my sister, flew all the way from Australia to be with us for part of it, and the treatment was in a very new and beautiful hospital for adults, which they opened especially for Toby on Saturday morning for his extra sixth day of treatment. Most adults undergoing treatment were visibly upset at the thought of children experiencing cancer and Toby made some very sweet older friends who would spoil him with cards and encouragement. The radiotherapists were also particularly kind and gentle. Toby and I played the lottery at the time with the numbers we received while waiting for his treatments. We were going to transform the children's hospital so that it could look like this beautiful new adult's cancer centre.

Unfortunately at the end of November 2009 the shunt wound, which ended up being in the line of fire of the radiotherapy treatment, became infected and re-opened. We rushed Toby into hospital again and in the operating theatre a new temporary drain was attached to his brain, requiring him once again to lie horizontally for almost a week. As soon as it was clear that the antibiotics were working and the infection was localized and maintained he had another operation to insert a new permanent shunt on the other side of his head. The very real danger of the infection spreading had thankfully been averted but Toby was still extremely weak and very seriously ill and required another three weeks in hospital. We wondered just how much Toby could withstand and marvelled at his fortitude and uncomplaining attitude.

Because of the intensive damage to the skin by radiotherapy the infected shunt wound was also not healing well and the viability nurse, a specialist nurse in wound healing, administered medicinal manuka honey to the site. I was so relieved to have a little of nature in her purity come to grace Toby's head.

Toby remained serenely resilient and resolute, and just before Christmas 2009 we got to take him home so that he could rebuild his strength, gain a few pounds and allow his wound to heal before the onslaught of a year of chemotherapy began. He looked like a ghost of himself.

The rest of my family, including Noah our eldest son, headed to my sister's wedding in Melbourne, Australia. I was supposed to have been my sister's maid of honour but instead Noah, just before his twelfth birthday, went with my parents and siblings to represent the four of us. It was so hard to say goodbye to Noah and allow him to fly to the other side of the world without us but I knew it was the right thing to do. He represented our family beautifully and had such a wonderful, life-affirming experience.

Toby, Ghislain and I stayed in Ireland alone over Christmas and bundled a very frail Toby into a motor home and set out on an adventure across wintery Ireland with Toby surveying the scenery from his bed. This was Toby's idea and he loved every second of it and announced before the departure that he did not want any mention of 'his' cancer. That was the first time he had even used the word, never mind appropriating it to himself.

Before departure we stayed a few days at home to prepare. Our house was very quiet as it was holiday time, and Toby was so weak he was unable to move. Instead of feeling alone I experienced a feeling of complete bliss surround me like a warm blanket for about two days. I had a clear and delicious sense of utter freedom from any form of belief which was such sweet relief and simultaneously disconcerting. I knew instinctively to trust the process. It was as if I was being emptied of any adherence to any particular way of being. Beliefs would arise in my consciousness almost as if presenting themselves for approval and I would acknowledge them and dismiss them when I could find no internal resonance to them.

Finally one thought recurred and has remained and it is the only belief that I felt able to accept at all. It is simple, "It is important to be kind; kind to oneself and to all of life." This was the beginning of my healing.

WISHES DO COME TRUE

As a child experiencing a life-threatening illness, Toby was eligible to receive a gift surprise from the charity `Make a Wish`. Toby was a great fan of Kobe Bryant, the famous basketball player for Los Angeles Lakers, and really wanted to meet him. The staff visiting from `Make a Wish` acknowledged Toby's wish but delicately asked him to consider a second wish because the charity was no longer able to fly children beyond Europe, and so meeting up with Kobe Bryant would, they believed, not be possible. They left Toby to think about another wish.

Toby was intransigent. He just could not find a second wish. His wish was to meet Kobe Bryant. I told him to believe completely and utterly in this wish, giving all his attention to it.

Three weeks later the staff from `Make a Wish` in London phoned, "You are not going to believe this but the LA Lakers are coming to London in October to play in a friendly with the Minnesota Timberwolves in the O2 arena, and we are trying to get tickets and arrange a meeting with Kobe after the match. This is going to be difficult and we may not know for sure that we will meet him until the day itself, so please do not say anything to Toby yet".

At the beginning of October 2010 his wish came true. The timing was perfect as Toby was finishing his sixth cycle of treatment and was not feeling as nauseous as he would have at the beginning of the cycle. We had a phenomenal weekend. `Make a Wish` lodged us in a central London hotel just behind the Tate Gallery and within walking distance of Westminster and Big Ben. Toby could not walk far at the time but I managed to sneak out to the Tate gallery with Noah which was such a treat. We all went to the zoo together and had a special guided tour of the Tower of London and the crown jewels, and my brother, who lives in London, was able to join us for some of the fun. On the night of the match we were whisked off in a limousine to the O2 Arena to watch the LA Lakers play the Minnesota Timberwolves. We found ourselves in the O2 arena, which seats twenty thousand people, sharing a corporate box with two other children and their families who had had the same wish as Toby. I remember taking in the whole exciting scene before our eyes and wondering how Toby`s dream had come true. I was awestruck at the majesty of such perfect synchronicity.

During one of the breaks the amazing Hall of Famer, James Worthy, came to visit us. James had played no. 42 for the Lakers so he signed Toby`s Kobe Bryant shirt on the four leaving room for Kobe to sign the shirt on the 2. We went down to the courtside to meet Kobe who was as equally gentle and gracious as James. He chatted to each of the families, and encouraged the kids to do what they love. "That`s the secret", he said. "Do what you love!" We bounced out of the arena that night.

PEOPLE POWER

The trip to London was just the boost we needed to face the following few months. As the treatments increased so did their accumulative effect and by the end we had such a fragile child in our hands. Toby would often go for days without food, and had already lost a third of his body weight.

It took almost eighteen months to complete all of Toby's treatment. We had had no MRI scans during the treatment as the scar tissue from treatment and interventions would have prevented a clear scan reading. The final MRI scan, following the end of treatment, was therefore an extremely important one that would indicate whether Toby was clear of cancer or not. If the cancer was still there the hospital had very little to offer us in terms of further treatment, so everything was hanging in the balance, and we felt it.

It took a painful two weeks and six days before the final results came in. Towards the end of the wait I became so desperate that I tried to find out why it was all taking so long and was told that the MRI scanner unit in the main adult hospital, where we had been scanned, was overwhelmed. There was a waiting list of seven months for the scan.

My two brothers and two cousins were about to do a Tough Guy contest so I sent an email to all of our friends, family and colleagues explaining the situation and asking them to sponsor my brothers and my cousins in their Tough Guy quest. The response was so positive that by the time the men had finished their gruelling ordeal the donations amounted to £8000. Five years later the MRI scanner is finally up and running in the children's hospital.

I was so impressed by people power. It felt like everyone was relieved to be able to help practically in some way and they showed this by donating so generously.

Three days after my email to our friends to ask for help, on the evening of 28ᵗʰ January 2011, Toby's oncologist phoned with the results. I could not speak to him as the relief poured out in one almighty sob. The following day I was able to share our good news.

Dear all,

We received Toby's results at six on Thursday evening when I was very much at the end of my tether.

His scan is clear and 'without residue'!

The sweetness of relief is huge and we are deeply grateful to life.

To every hand that has touched Toby, to every heart that has felt for him and for every fervent prayer that was uttered with us in mind, we are deeply appreciative.

None of us know what the next moment will bring but there is no moment as large and wide, as broad and beautiful as a moment of total and utter gratitude.

Much love and thanks to you all for being there for us.

Please keep us on your prayer list.

AND SO MUM, ARE YOU STILL AFRAID OF DEATH?

During that three week wait for the results it was very difficult to not succumb to worry as our options seemed so limited and utterly dependent upon a clear result. Toby obviously sensed it. One night as I went to tuck him into bed I arrived to find him lying very still with the covers over his head. I remember pausing at the door and thinking in a very detached way, "well this is how it will be. He will just lie very still and there will be no more Toby". As I approached his bed I noticed that he had made a cardboard cut-out of a tombstone which he had placed on top of the duvet covering his face. It read `Toby, R.I.P`.

I shuddered but could find no words and so hugged him tight, said our good night prayers and left him to sleep. The following night as I came to put him to sleep I came upon the same scenario but this time his cardboard cut-out was more elaborate. It read:

His name in full, R.I.P,

In God we trust (which he had copied from an American dollar note)

And finally at the bottom he had written his age, which he had calculated in years, months and days to that very moment.

The following day I managed to slip out into my town and, by chance, met with a teacher, from the local Rudolf Steiner School, who I knew would help me find clarity. I told her what had happened at bedtime with Toby the previous two evenings and, without missing a beat, she suggested that we simply talk about death. She felt Toby was trying to initiate that discussion.

For the next two weeks whenever I got a relaxed opportunity I talked about my grandparents' death. I reminded both boys of how Noah, when he was four, and Toby two, had insisted that we stay in the graveyard at the funeral of my paternal grandfather until everyone else had left and it was only us, the coffin, the grave, and the gravediggers remaining. Noah had been cross with me for wearing black at the time and had asked me why. I could not give him a better reason than that is what we do. Noah asked the gravediggers if Toby and he could help bury their great-grandfather. The gravediggers found two very small spades for both Noah and Toby, and as they threw soil on the coffin a bird swooped down over the grave. I was struck at the time by Noah's determination to pay homage to a generation departed. At such a young age he was aware of how precious and joyful the gift of life is, which is why, I believe, he scolded me for wearing such a joyless colour as black.

I also spoke to Noah and Toby of how I had been present at my maternal grandmother's deathbed; their great-grandmother. We had celebrated her 100th birthday party just three months before her death and now she was dying consciously with her family around her. She was dignified and strong throughout the night as her body began to shut down. As morning came she was still hanging on and we felt that she was waiting for her son, a priest, to return from Rome in time for her death. We phoned him to Rome to speak with her as early as we could in the morning. He told her what the readings had been at mass and reminded her of how devoted she had been to Jesus and especially Mary in her prayers and how they would be waiting for her, and as he spoke, she looked up and took her last breath. I remember telling Toby how I saw Granny slip easily from her body, and how strange it was to look upon her body after death and know that she was no longer there.

I told Toby too of how I had felt the presence of my paternal grandmother who had died when I was twenty-two. Eight years later, when I was standing by the window in our apartment in Abu Dhabi with Toby as a very small baby in my arms, she appeared by my side, smiling warmly at me and looking lovingly at him.

After about two weeks of these stories I met Toby in the stairwell coming down towards me. As we met he said benevolently, "And so mum, are you still afraid of death?"

I knew that this question, although completely unexpected, was the culmination of our discussions, and I needed to get it right.

"No Toby. I'm not afraid of death but I'm absolutely not ready! I have too much to experience, too much to see and too much to do. But when the moment comes I know I'll be ready and I won't be scared."

Toby nodded slowly with a smile and said, "Very good mum", and continued on down the stairs.

YOU`RE MY MUM YOU KNOW...AND THAT`S ENOUGH

There were moments like these with my two boys when I wondered who was teaching who. I am sure that most mums and dads have moments when the higher spirit of their child shines through and you hear, as if in stereo, its great wisdom. I particularly love this aspect of parenting when age and maturity become irrelevant in that moment of sharing.

There were times also when I felt Toby was reading my thoughts, "You're a mum mum: there are anxious mums, frustrated mums, cross mums, tired mums but you're a mum mum." This was the first time I had been declared fit for purpose by my second son. It felt like the culminating point after many weeks, months, years of me not quite hitting the mark. He had just celebrated his tenth birthday and for weeks previously had been calling out to me regularly from every corner of the house, "You're my mum, you know!" Sometimes

I would remain silent pondering the significance of this obvious statement. Other times I would just hug him or reply "I know I'm your mum, aren't I the lucky one? And you're my Toby, you know".

It was a curious statement and part of me wondered if he was just trying to acknowledge my crucial role in his life or was he trying to stake a further claim on my time. I asked him once why he always said this to me, and he answered, "Other people say to their mums, I love you, but I say, you're my mum".

I had been off work for almost two years, and Toby was very slowly returning to school and I was wrestling again with the thought of dipping my foot back into my professional world, if only to attend two weekends of training. Yogabuddies, my yoga organization, was my creation, and I was torn, leaving it uncared for. I was thinking about the future and my 'career' as a yoga teacher and was feeling the urge to validate that with further training to help me get back into teaching. This is when Toby's lyrical litany had begun, "You're my mum, you know".

So I had finally got to the place where I had decided not to go to the trainings as I knew it was not truly what I was in need of at that moment. I announced this decision to my mother, and noted a smile of satisfaction on Toby's face.

My own personal sense of satisfaction with this decision was short lived as I was feeling so cut off from normal life. As I was standing making myself a cup of tea I was *again* wondering in my own little head, not out loud, "What am I to do with myself, what is my life's passion, what can I offer this world, how can I make my mark?"

And from the lounge came the words, "You're my mum you know… and that is enough".

Was this child hearing my thoughts?

It *was* enough to be his mum because that was a full time job as it was, just caring daily for him, and advocating for him in school. Although his treatment had ended he had been left wounded. We had to watch out for his shunt becoming blocked which required us always to be within two and half hours of the hospital. He needed bi-lateral hearing aids as the chemotherapy and radiotherapy had damaged his high tone hearing and left him moderately deaf. His balance was still off kilter and he had suffered a sixth nerve cerebral palsy which meant he had been left with a squint in one eye and was experiencing double vision. He also had nystagmus on extremes of gaze. He was suffering quite debilitating nausea and was dependent on medication for cortisol, thyroxine and growth hormone deficiency as the radiotherapy had damaged his pituitary gland. And so although thankfully he had survived, he was sore from battle.

BATTLE WEARY

The news of a clear scan was truly wonderful and everyone was so thrilled for us but we were, at the same time, all battle weary, and were being faced with having to redefine ourselves and our lives. There was very little preparation for Toby to go back to school. He was just encouraged to get back in there as soon as possible but he felt so weak, nauseous and off balance, and the extent of his hearing loss only became apparent when he was not able to hear what his teacher was saying or what the class members were whispering to him to help him out. The difficulties in adaptation to a new way of life were becoming evident to us but I still had to make a plea for extra help at school and challenge the authorities when the extra help was removed without warning two years later after his successful entrance to grammar school. This was soul destroying because in my mind Toby was stronger and more amazing than ever and deserved every bit of help that could be given him. I had thought the hardest part of Toby's life would be his cancer treatment but going back to school and taking stock of his limitations, hidden and apparent, was just as challenging.

I was also feeling that this life event, Toby's illness, was shaking me so deeply to the core that I was not able to `go back` to what I was before it. Nothing outside home was resonating with me and it was sometimes just downright uncomfortable to be in company. I was very much in no man's land, and no other man or woman could make it right.

A HEALING VISIT

Although painful, I knew at a soul level that this whole experience was the opportunity to bring healing to myself, as well as Toby, and that we were in this together, and that my healing would be his and his, mine.

My Higher Office had told me:

> You call to your experience everything that you have so thought to desire, everything that you have so feared to live.

I knew that I was in the full throes of that process, the `Great Homecoming` my Higher Self had spoken of; the bringing home to myself of all those emotions that I so feared to face like terror, separation, despair, grief, loss, self-judgement, and all I could do was to keep going on with the belief that I would get the help to navigate it all. The process was not particularly graceful. I did a lot of resisting, doubting, mourning, complaining and worrying, and so many times I was just so tired and wanted to give up not knowing when I would be "done with it all".

In equal measure though, I also did a lot of surrendering to and nurturing of myself. Every part of my wounded self asked to be seen, held, nurtured and accepted, and I knew this was my time to do it. The end was not in sight and many times I felt like I was going around in circles but I knew it had to get easier at some point, and I also knew that when I asked for help from my Higher Office or Heaven or my angels or guides, help would come.

To begin to really heal I knew that I had to allow all parts of me to be loved. I had to let unconditional love penetrate every aspect of my humanness. I had to let it into the deepest and darkest recesses of my very being so that it could shine its light upon me and embrace me in its fullness. And those recesses were so hard to reveal even to myself because they were my endless self-judgements and criticisms.

I prayed earnestly and incessantly that I could love myself completely. On one particular day I was walking swiftly through our lounge to the office where I had a lot of administrative work awaiting me. As I crossed the threshold into the lounge I was, without warning, met by a presence of love that was so overpowering in its gentleness, acceptance and complete unconditional love that my knees buckled and I fell to the floor. I was looked at by this presence with such exquisite fraternal love that I felt all my resistance melt. It was a perfect moment in time and one that I can recall vividly.

NO ROOM FOR CRITICISM

I wish I could say that I always feel this unconditional love for myself; I do not. Nor can I claim that I am a master of anything that is shared through the writings in this book. I am a messenger, and a continual student of learning, who messes up regularly. But I know now that messing up is part of the deal and that to judge myself in any way is to weaken my strength, as my Higher Office explains.

> Know that you are strong and that you have a strength that is vaster, deeper, wider and more inexhaustible than you can imagine. Just know that this strength will take you everywhere, even calmly through death when you face it.

> In the recognition of this strength there is no need to fear for you will always move forward and through any challenge that comes your way.

> The secret is not to be critical of yourself in the process. Just keep acknowledging your strength. You have access to a strength that makes you highly effective. Trust in your strength and your beauty of spirit. Trust that all is well and constantly unfolding for the good of all.

So I can only keep trying, knowing that I am enough and that I am love and that love can embrace all things. When I feel my heart heavy or when tears rise to the surface I can remind myself to embrace them completely and wholly. I can breathe them into my fingers, breathe them into my toes. I can give myself the time to be still and I can call out for help with faith that help will come. I can also fully embrace the joy and happiness that is life, simple delicious pleasures like being together in front of the fire with my family or running along the coast.

I know now that nothing is sent to punish me or imprison me, and that I am truly innocent because if I knew how to be better or act better I would be doing it. I know that life, even when it can seem harsh and unbearable, is there ultimately to liberate me, and when I fully embrace myself throughout all that life brings what I will discover will make me wiser and more compassionate of myself and others. I know also now that the real learning does not uniquely come on high from angelic voices but is in the everyday challenges, joys and harsh truths we have to face.

THE POWER OF CREATING ANEW

As Toby finally begins to thrive again, I can only be so profoundly grateful that we get to be with him and enjoy life together.

I am deeply grateful to Ghislain, my husband, who is a dynamic creator. Throughout Toby's illness he has constantly pushed us to create anew in countless ways but especially in the planting of our edible forest garden and the rebuilding of our home, which we somehow managed to do through this experience.

There is great healing and empowerment in creating anew. As my Higher office says:

> This is your task as an alchemist; to transform all that you see and all that you are with by the loving regard you hold in its favour. It is that simple. Beauty is in the eye of the beholder. Behold all that you see with love. Purify this look of love for all that comes into your life. That is where the mastery lies.

And so enlightenment or whatever you wish to call it: coming to awareness or growing in consciousness is not, I think, what I hoped it to be; an exit card of grace to constant pure bliss and joy. It is instead, I am coming to believe, and this is a *big instead*, the practice of complete and total acceptance of every experience that comes to my door knowing that I am a creator and that through the power of love I can transform all that I see and all that I am.

GIVE YOURSELF THE LOVE THAT YOU SEEK

When I breathe any emotion fully into my fingers and toes now, I know that I am bringing it into the fullness of me, the fullness and completeness of the love that I am. I am bringing it home so that it can complete its task and in doing so enrich my compassion for myself and for others. I cannot be overwhelmed because I am the love that I seek and in that love everything finds resolution. As they explain:

> When you are in the grasp of an emotion do not try to figure it out. Move into a place of deliberate stillness and move to the core of the love that you are. Try not to search it from outside yourself but imagine this furnace of love just below where you imagine your heart to be. It is a stove of love designed to help you traverse the most difficult terrain. It is a hearth of love, comfort and nurture and reminds you that you are love, you are light, you are safety and you are beautiful, and out of all situations that you may find yourself in there are only the most loving of solutions to choose from. Just know that you are well. Give yourself the love that you seek. Give yourself the security that you yearn. Give yourself the abundance that you covet. Give yourself the time that you require to feel at peace within yourself.

MY WISH

I do not logically know where the messages in this book come from, other than that I receive them from somewhere other than my head. As soon as I begin to write, my restlessness and fears are calmed and I begin to feel the love and compassion in these messages woo and amuse me. I feel my Higher Office send their love, their good humour, their wit and their encouragement on every word. As I was about to edit this work for publishing I asked for their help and they replied,

Hold the cloth, dear one, while we embroider.

In all things, may I hold the cloth, trusting that all is well and that everything is working out for the highest good of all.

If we can just know ourselves to be loved and capable of love then we can move mountains.

Believe in your ability to be in love; that is the key.

May the words in this book be a pulsating reminder of the love that we are learning to know ourselves to be.

Jane-Louise

Holywood,
September 2016

Part One

QUITE A WONDROUS AFFAIR

You know this blessed earthly journey is really quite a wondrous affair. Your full glory is hidden from your eyes so that you may make the journey back to the wonderment and awe of who you are. Humanity is now in this process. So much love is being poured out to you to help you remember your divinity. For every human there is an army of spirit beings ready to help. Please urge your fellow divine humans to remember that help is always there. This will help make their journey less onerous and bring them back to the joy that is so rightfully theirs.

Over the next years of your time we are going to come to the most marvellous of discoveries and each discovery will bring you closer to love, for love is the Holy Grail. This experience of love is what you are here to discover, it is not more complicated than that. If you can keep this one thought in mind then your life will become a layered cake of the most delectable kind and you will lick your fingers with the sheer pleasure of being alive.

To really live is to be able to create in every moment of your existence, and love will help you, indeed enable you to transcend all that limits you and scares you and hinders you from being all that you are and can be. There is great excitement here for the many discoveries you are to make. Do you feel it?

Believe in your ability to be in love; that is the key.

THE CAVERNOUS HEART

We would have you know that each one of you is the most glorious beaming angel, full of divine sparkling diamonds of wisdom and beauty. You are glorious beyond your imagination and you have simply forgotten. Take a deep breath, and another, and yet again and go deep into your heart space. Inside this heart space is a cavern and within this cavern is a fire burning which brings light and warmth. Sit down by this fire and warm yourself. Watch the flames dance and feel this dance within your soul. Watch intently and imagine yourself to be part of the flame. When you are ready, stand up again and move deeper into this high ceiling vaulted cavern where very soon you will come across a door on your right, open it and walk in. This is the dressing chamber where you can remove those old smoky clothes and allow yourself to be dressed in brilliant white clothes presented to you by your angels.

Before donning your new clothes dip yourself in the warm baths prepared for your tired body. Listen to the echo of the movement of the water in this vaulted chamber and feel the softness of the water on your skin. Loll deliciously in this soft water and feel its warmth and love as it caresses your body. As you lie in this water imagine the beauty and perfection of your physical vessel and enjoy its splendour. You are a child of God, a spark of pure light that has its origin in the

God Creator of all. You are a droplet of the Creator's inspiration and love and its desire to manifest its magnificence. Allow this reality to penetrate your very being and your very soul. May you be loved and blessed, honoured and cherished.

A FIELD OF PURPLE HEATHER

We would have you close your eyes again and imagine yourself in an extended field of purple heather. It is soft under foot, buoying you up, and the sky above is blue with one or two clouds floating by. Take off your rucksack and lie down on this earthly bed prepared with you in mind. Allow yourself to be supported as you imagine each plant jostle for the honour of supporting your human body. They see you as an angel and are delighted that you would spend time with them. With the confidence of knowing that you are safe and cherished in this outdoor place, allow your eyes to close, your breath to lengthen and your cares to leave you. Very soon the birds of the sky make their presence felt. They will not come too close for fear of startling you but they watch with wonderment as a human 'being' takes time out from 'doing' to simply be with them in this space of nature that is the greatest gift available from God Creator.

Listen to the song of these heavenly beings as they swoop in freedom in the sky. Know too that your heart sings in accompaniment and pulses with the universal energy that allows you to be as one. Know too beloved 'being' that in this safe space every animal present in that field knows that you are there 'being'. Each one has synchronized its breathing to match the vibration of your heart which has harmonized with the heartbeat of Mother Earth. In this safe space your divinity is shining out in rays of pure love and light because you have simply sought out the safe space in the bosom of Mother Earth, and in this moment she is cherishing and loving you like no other mother could.

Feel her love. Do her the honour of not scorning her gift. Do her the honour of accepting her love with open arms and an open heart. The gift may be the most precious one you have ever received. Have courage in every thought. Do not miss a single heartbeat of love that comes as a gift of life to you.

PLEASURE

Pleasure is a beautiful word. See in it the word *please*, to please oneself, one's Higher Self, and so with it all the heavenly realms. Do you know that when you are giving yourself pleasure the whole Universe sings with you? 'Ure' pleasing of yourself brings the pleas-*ure* to all those that surround you and who are with you in Spirit. Your initial blueprint was programmed to live in joy. Your free will allowed you the freedom to step out of this natural condition and experience other parts of the spectrum of the emotional world. Each emotion is a planet onto itself. How many have you visited? Have you enjoyed your adventures there? What planets do you intend to hop to and from today?

We invite you to the planet of 'please yourself'. This pleasing of yourself does not mean that you deny others of pleasure through indulging your own pleasure, so do not carry this worry. Your deep pleasure is the rumbling earthquake that blasts open, with joy and abandon, the portals of pleasure and joy lying dormant in those around you.

On this planet of pleasure the birds sing their song of love to you, the plants sway in rhythm to your heartbeat, the sun shines rays of healing light and the moon bathes you in its magic. All that surrounds you sways in the magic of your being and delights in the pleasure of life itself.

We love you and laugh with you when you laugh. Your laugh echoes through the highways and byways of the Universe. Your smile lights up the stars of the heavens and your cheeriness reaches those whose heart is heavy with the forgetting of the joy that lies dormant within their very being. Come to the planet of pleasure, leave your worries aside and bask in the state of being that is so rightfully yours.

THE FRUIT OF THE ROSE

Welcome again to the table of fruit; succulent juicy fruit. Pick up a piece, choose well and then bite into it. Feel the strength of your teeth, the elasticity of your mouth, the sense buds on your tongue and the texture of the fruit; all in one bite! Can you imagine that this is life? Bite into it! Do not be afraid that it will taste sour. Simply choose your experience and then savour every moment. If it is too sour and you have not chosen in your greatest light then just spit out this mouthful and try again. The basket is full to overflowing with the most delicious types of fruit and they are there simply so that you may taste them. Do not hesitate.

Become like a child about to open a present, feel the anticipation and the trust that it will be all that you have dreamed of and more. Life is a bowl of fruit! It is a heavenly gift and we know you will taste it with relish, with honour, with truth, and offer it to yourself as the divine gift it is. And in return it will feed you, nourish you, nurture you and enliven you. And then, oh yes then, the fruit of the rose will blossom.

THE ETERNAL GARDEN

Once upon a time there was a beautiful old man with white hair, a wizened face with each wrinkle telling the story of a bygone age. He had a large garden full of the most beautiful flowers, fruit trees, nut trees, animals of all different shapes and sizes. There were boats floating gently along the rivers and waterfalls cascading joyously from on high. In the centre of this world of utter perfection there was an ancient tree. Many people would come and sit under this tree to take shelter from the elements. Many a happy picnic was celebrated under this tree and many a joyful child skipped around it or played hide and seek in it. It was an idyllic scene.

Until one day the old man decided he did not want anybody else to come into his garden and he closed it up with lock and key. The people were distraught. They could hear the birds singing from the other side of the grand wall that separated them from this garden. How they mourned the loss of their freedom in this garden.

They began to dislike the wizened old man. They began even to curse him and feel very badly done by and their lives began to reflect their anger. They felt abandoned and unloved and could not understand.

Outside the walls of this garden it was also very beautiful but the people did not feel as secure and as loved outside the walls as they did inside. They thought the old man had been cruel to them and they sat for a long time on their stone seats feeling hurt.

The children however became impatient sitting on their stone seats, and as their parents sat mourning the loss of the garden, the children began to play. As they played they discovered the most wonderful old trees to hide behind which reminded them of the ancient tree in their former garden.

They kept on playing, and in their search for places to hide they began to discover what seemed like an eternal garden.

And by and by they were no longer angry at the Old Man because they realized that outside their former garden was an even bigger garden to play in.

And so it is for you. The Father sent you away to play and discover and rediscover. And it is indeed an eternal pursuit that will lead you in the ever-expanding pursuit of love.

LOVE IS...

Love is such a delicious state of being. It is free from judgement, criticism, fear and feels like a warm blanket inside. Thoughts that do not nourish you, have no place in your mind. There is no room for self-doubt or incrimination or judgement or criticism or second-guessing.

We will give you an image. Say that you are standing on a mountain side and you can see the summit far away. One tiny little rain cloud fills what is otherwise a pristine blue sky and you say to yourself, "Oh no, there is going to be a big rainstorm. I am not going to get to the summit today!" And yet if you just kept walking, admiring the blue sky and the warmth of the sun, you would be at the summit within a question of a few hours having enjoyed a most beautiful walk. "Ah", you say to yourself, "the rain cloud will get me on the way down". Maybe indeed it will, but it will bring the most refreshing raindrops to cool you down from the ardour of the sun. Do you see? This world is as benevolent as you wish it to be.

YOUR CURRICULUM VITAE

Fill your heart with the knowledge that all is in perfect motion towards the realization of your dreams and desires. We do not take your requests lightly. As soon as your expression is accompanied with the truth and passion of 'All That You Are', the wheels are set in motion. The third element is trust and that is where you need to be in every moment.

You live in a body that is nothing short of miraculous. With every heartbeat your whole system breathes life. This is one of the greatest gifts of life. How can you doubt for one second the magnificence of a Universe that, in all its love, wants what you want for yourself? You have deciphered what you want through your own truth, and we feel your passion, so now we ask you to trust.

This life is impassioning, and it is through your own personal fulfilment and joy that you begin to allow others around you to blossom. We are all in the process of realizing Heaven on Earth. We have experienced the alternatives and now as a planet and as a realm of the Universe we are ready to raise our vibrations to one of unadulterated love.

Can you imagine your curriculum vitae in this new energy?

Name: Light of Love.

Address: The Undulating Universe of Euphoria.

Age: As old and as young as the illusion of time.

Civil Status: As free as the birds which grace the sky.

Experience: Aeons of time that have brought me thus far on the cusp of all-empowering love.

Career development: Within every breath I envision the potential of `All That Is` and, as I do, we meld into one.

Projected salary: I live in a universe of abundance where `All That Is` fulfils my every need before I can even express it.

We welcome you to the service of `All That Is`. The only punch-in card you will need here is to take the breath of life and live in the trust that you are forever loved, cherished and taken care of. We love you with the wings of light itself. As you sleep we buoy you up on the downy feathers of comfort and compassion. We tickle your passion, your love of life and reignite your desire to be of joyful service to the creator of `All That Is`.

We take our leave of this page but know that you are never alone.

THE TOOTHLESS CROCODILE

Once upon a time there was a crocodile. This was a special kind of crocodile because he had no teeth. In fact he was the only crocodile in the whole pond that had no teeth. You know, he may have even been the only crocodile in the whole swamp of ponds that had no teeth.

It might have been very annoying for this crocodile to be toothless but in fact he considered it a blessing of sorts because all the other crocodiles in this pond took pity on him and shared their food with him. They even mashed up the meat they caught for themselves in their large fierce jaws and they munched and munched so that all the toothless crocodile needed to do was swallow. And so this toothless crocodile would sit every day in his favourite part of the swamp and eat the food that was prepared for him by the other crocodiles. He really enjoyed his privileged position!

Until one day there was a storm and it rained and rained and rained. It rained so hard and for so long that the level of the water in the ponds increased. It increased so much that the ponds began to join up and finally became one big pond and the toothless crocodile found himself in a big ocean of ponds. It was so big that he was separated from his crocodile family that used to help him so much. This big toothless crocodile began to panic because he could not imagine how we was going to survive without teeth in this big ocean of ponds, and without anyone to catch his food and chew it up for him. It had been so long since he had gone in search of his own food that he was afraid even to try. He was afraid even to open his mouth. He had, in fact, forgotten how to feed himself.

For three long weeks he went without food. He would see all sorts of fish pass by but he dared not open his jaws until he finally got so hungry that he found a quiet little place in this ocean of ponds and he lay low and just opened his wide toothless jaws in the hope that something would swim into them.

By and by little fish swam into his jaws and swam right down into his tummy. There were so many that they nourished him fully and all he had to do was sit and wait very quietly for them, trusting that some would swim right into his open jaws.

Weeks went by and the toothless crocodile finally began to find a way to live in this new ocean. He sometimes missed the meat prepared by his crocodile family but now he knew that, toothless or not, he would never go hungry again!

In times of change you will have moments of feeling 'toothless'. It will feel like the rug has been pulled from underneath your feet. Find a comfortable place in this great sea of motion and wait with your heart open for the spiritual manna you search. This 'feeding time' will give you the nourishment, you need, to swim in freedom and courage in this deeper ocean. Peace to you.

THE OLD MAN AND OLD WOMAN

Once upon a time there was an old man and an old woman who lived in part of a remote field at the top of a hill. Their mothers and fathers had lived on this hill and the mothers and fathers of their mothers and fathers had lived on the top of this hill.

It so happened that one day a whole entourage of very elegant people passed by in a line of majestic-looking carriages along the bottom wall of their field. The man straightened up from the digging of his potatoes and called to the old woman to come away from the washing line to take a good look at what was happening.

In the line-up were carriages of gold and silver, drawn by lavishly decorated horses. Each carriage was driven by finely liveried drivers and within each one sat such regal looking people. The old man and old woman really could not imagine what such beautiful people were doing in this part of the country, driving past their field and their hill. Nobody ever came this way except the odd visitor delivering news from afar.

It suddenly occurred to the old man of the hill to put down his spade and walk down the field to the wall to have a closer look, and so they both did. In anticipation but also for fear that he would miss the whole affair, he broke into a little jog towards the bottom of the field and his old wife did the same. Gosh, they had not gone much faster than at walking pace for quite a while. They had nothing to fear however for as they got closer to the wall and looked down the lane they could see no end to this fanciful train of splendid horse-drawn carriages.

They stood for what felt like ages waving to the people in each of the carriages until one carriage finally stopped and out stepped the most beautiful lady and gentleman that either the old man or old woman had ever set eyes upon. The beauty of this gentleman and lady was so astounding that the old man and old woman fell to their knees in awe and honour. They simply could not help themselves. As the old man and old woman knelt with their heads to the ground they very soon felt the presence of this glorious couple behind them beckoning them to come up the hill.

This time it was as if they floated up the hill. And as they came to the top of their hill they stopped and looked around. And although, like their ancestors, they had lived all their lives in this same place, it was as if they were seeing the view for the first time and how splendid it was. It was as if they were seeing the glint of sun on the leaves of the trees for the first time. It was as if they were hearing the bubbling of the brook for the first time. It was as if they were noticing the expanse of the layout of the fields and their neat stone walls for the first fresh time.

And as they stood in appreciation of the exquisite perfection of all that lay before them they turned to look back in thanks to the beautiful couple. But when they turned back there was no one to be seen. The train of splendid horse-drawn carriages had also disappeared. In astonishment they turned to look at each other but how much greater was their amazement when they saw in each other the beautiful man and beautiful woman looking back at them.

Know that when you take time to notice and admire the beauty around you, it will become as if it is your own.

THE UNBRIDLED HORSE

Once upon a time there was a horse that had no master. Every morning this horse would throw up its head and gallop along and over every byway in the countryside without a care. He was heedless, unharnessed, unkempt, unloved but he considered himself free and did not look for a home. He was wild and loved to be in the wild.

Until one day, after much travelling through the country, he came finally to a cliff edge and it felt like he was at the furthest end of the world and there was nowhere more to go. He was not a seahorse and he did not consider plunging into the sea below. He was wild but not altogether senseless. He stayed in the field by the edge of the cliff for a few days and then trotted on to the other fields and byways that bordered this cliff edge. He began to enjoy living on the cliff edge. He began to feel King of the Cliff Edge, and it gave him a feeling of expansion to be able to contemplate the horizon and a whole vista of watery universe that he knew he could not be part of, unless he was ready to plunge to his death. This horse was beginning to enjoy the fact that he could just keep walking alongside the cliff and enjoy being there at the edge.

He soon became well known and all the people on the island where he lived knew that, at some time of the year, the wild horse would be passing along their coastline and they did all they could to nurture him as he passed by their way.

The horse grew less wild as he trotted along the coast. The edge of this great expansion had finally fettered his wild ways, and the contemplation of a universe beyond the edge gave the horse much to ruminate upon.

Years went by and this horse carved out a pathway for himself all along the large island, which was used by many. The wild horse made many friends and had many places of repose and respite where he could simply be in front of the great expanse of sea.

Until one day, after many years of cliff-edge walking, the path gave way and the wild horse fell into this great sea of expansion and contemplation. As he fell through the air he felt more exhilaration than fear. It was as if his view of the expanse of sea was widening before him. So liberating was this feeling that instead of joining this expanse he felt himself sprouting wings and before he knew it his wings were flapping with an astounding power that gave him lift. The joy in his heart was immense and the feeling of freedom exhilarating. He swooped and glided on the wings of the wind. He soared and he dropped into the down winds. He flew towards the horizon and back to land. He flew as high as he could and as low as he dared. He was King of the Air. After much fun flying the horse came back to the coast where all those that loved him waited in astonished silence. Gently he landed by them reassuring them that he was fine and that his fledgling wings were giving him much joy. He offered to take some of his friends for a ride. One or two dared to accept and were so exhilarated on their return that they wanted to sprout wings of their own. Many flocked to the coast to witness for themselves the flying horse.

The horse no longer took the worn path. Now he flew all over the country and over the land and even to different lands and was known for his wisdom, courage and love.

Let the winds of change blow out the cobwebs that stick diligently to the corners of your being. Take, with us, the wind of breath that in its utter simplicity, purity and devotion blows through your being infusing it with the pure love that is your divine birthright. Imagine flying and soaring above this world. You know that at any time you can alight and be on land again but adopt this feeling of expansion and flight and become accustomed to living your life with wings. We are giving you these wings.

You did not fall into the abyss. You fell into the wings of change and the sea of motion. You were not crushed by the powerful waves nor did you fall onto the jagged rocks. No, you sprouted wings. Do not go back to land and hide them; shake them out. Yes we know they are quite expansive but you have far to travel and much to see and great heights to soar to. Let us fly on the wings of your breath.

ALLOW THE WIND TO BLOW THROUGH YOU

You are feeling and hearing the winds of change. For some it will trigger fear and cynicism, for others it will be the pathway to expansion and love. You do not need to go into fear anymore; these winds are here to exhilarate you, enliven you and love you.

Let us help each other by breathing in the love of Creator. As you breathe the breath of life it brings with it what feels like a tornado of new energy to every cell. It shakes the cell up, reminding it that it is the cell of life. It jiggles it and caresses it and plays with it and asks it to waken up and shine. That is happening when you breathe in the breath of life. It is the tornado of love that sweeps through your body dislodging what it is teetering in imbalance and bringing to expansion all that is ready to shine.

Sometimes the petals of the flower are blown off in the wind but only because they are ready to fly elsewhere on the breeze, and then new petals grow. Sometimes the whole flower dies and needs to re-root and grow from the bottom up again, and this can take a little effort. But most importantly this flower needs to be exposed to the elements, to grow and learn from them so that it can bend in the wind and withstand the pelting of heavy raindrops on a spring day or even bounce back up from being trampled on by a large inconsiderate foot.

THE BEDRIDDEN YOUNG GIRL

Once upon a time there was a young girl. She was joyful and free in her movements and her pastime was filled with the wonder of all that was around her. Every morning after breakfast she would throw open the door and, no matter what the weather, she would run into her garden whistling for the birds which, without fear, would approach her in the sweet expectation of receiving some titbit of food and a little fresh water in which they could bathe themselves. Never did the little girl miss this daily ritual. She relished the fresh air in her lungs. She loved to smell the air, guessing what the weather would do that day. She loved to feel the caress of the wind or the soft rain on her cheeks and in her hair. It was often simply a few minutes but it would allow her the time to connect with all that was around her.

Until one day it came in her young life to suffer from an illness. This illness so disturbed her that she lay for many days and even weeks in her little bedroom above the garden and her only connection with the outside was through her bedroom window. Every morning her mother would open the window so that the bedridden girl could hear the birds and smell the fresh air and see the clouds and guess what the weather would bring that day. As soon as the fresh morning air would hit the little girl's nostrils she would lie back on her pillow feeling refreshed and rewarded for the effort. She knew that within the air was held the secret of life. She knew that the purity and life-giving source within the air would penetrate every cell in her body, bringing sustenance and life and love. She knew that her healing was contained within every deep breath she took. And as the little girl lay in her bed she came to know that this breath of fresh air was her daily medicine.

She began to savour the smell, the texture, the humidity, the lightness, the heaviness, the expansiveness of this blast of air coming from the window. After three or four weeks of lying in her bed unable to move she knew simply from her morning breath of fresh air what the weather was like, what the earth was saying to her, how the birds were feeling, what stage of development the earth was at. And she honoured her sickness because she knew that it had brought a new level of learning, a new appreciation of life. While her body lay incapacitated, all her senses had become alive to all that is in 'All That Is'. And very soon her body became renewed.

Let this earth realm speak to your heart. Let the trees whisper to your being, let the budding of the flowers inspire you to push through the soil, let the flight of the birds lift your heart skywards, let the freshness of the air penetrate every breathing sac of your being and fill it with life in abundance.

Every day this little girl's mother opened the window for her. Mother Earth does the same for you. Let her love, her devotion and all her gifts penetrate your very soul so that you may rise from your bed and race out once more into the garden of life.

THE BANJO PLAYER

Once upon a time there was a young man with a banjo. He would play this banjo day and night. He would take it up to the top of the hill and play all alone until the sun would set behind him. His fingers would never tire and his heart would sing along with the melodies. It was his life. Everything else was fitted in around his banjo playing. He loved to share his joy with others and there would often be a ceilidh or two that he would play at. The girls would admire him and he did not run from their advances, and yet his only true love was his banjo.

Until one day, as he was cutting the hay with his father and brothers he caught his hand in the machinery and his precious banjo fingers were mangled and torn, bruised and burned. The pain in his hand was immense but the breaking of his heart shattered crystals in the very core of his being. He was devastated. His banjo playing was to be no more.

The pain became unbearable, the loss immense, and despite all the care and comforting possible from all those around him, this young man lost the will to live. He mourned the banjo that sat untouched in the corner of the parlour. Days became weeks, weeks became months and the sadness began to penetrate his home and the community. The healers were brought in, the doctors visited, but the mangled hand was not for saving.

One night when the banjo player lay weeping in his bed, the moonlight shone right onto his cheek and the sound of music filled his head and his heart. It was the sweetest music he had ever heard. It not only moved his heart but his very soul began to dance in the moonlight. He could not help himself and stood up from the bed bathed in this moonlight and began to move his body to the rhythm of the music of love. After many hours of dancing he finally fell into a deep slumber under the covers of his bed.

The following morning he awakened to a new feeling in his body. It was a lightness that he had never experienced. He walked to the parlour and as he looked at his banjo it began to play all by itself. It played the music of love. The strings plucked themselves and strummed rhythms and melodies the boy had only dreamed of.

The boy's heart exploded in an outburst of delight and joy. He lifted his banjo and hugged it to his heart. He knew now that it was not the playing of his banjo that he mourned but its sweet lovely music, and now the banjo was gifting him with the music, that with all his love, he had given to it.

The banjo continued to play and the music soothed and enlivened all those that had the honour of hearing its music. This boy toured the country and the world with the banjo that sang the song of love.

THE BULGING FISH

Once upon a time there was a bulging fish. He was *bulging* because he simply never stopped eating. He ate everything in his way; plankton, algae, seaweed, littler fish. He just did not know when to stop. Munch, munch, munch, burp, burp, burp. There was no room for anything else in his life but eating. Even when he was bubbling away to other fish he could hardly spend the time with them to find out how they were as he was already thinking about his next meal. Burp, burp, burp, munch, munch, munch.

Many meals later this fish began to have a stomach ache. At first he thought it was hunger. Having never been hungry of course in his short life he did not really know how that felt, so he decided to have more to eat just in case but even during the small pauses of not eating this bulging fish felt the stomach ache. He decided to change his diet, eat more little fish rather than the slimy algae! So he tried that for a few days but no improvement there. He tried swimming a little faster after those littler fish he wanted to eat but still his stomach ached. He finally decided that drastic measures were necessary and he set off to visit the Wise Old Fish. Munch, munch, munch, swim, swim, swim, burp, burp, burp.

The Wise Old Fish was exceptionally busy that day and the bulging fish would have to wait his turn. The stomach ache ached and the bulging fish became so out of sorts that he had to find a little crevasse in the rocks of the reef in search of some respite from the pain. He pushed himself further and further into the crevasse. Further and further he went and the pressure from the walls of the crevasse was so great that he could no longer feel his stomach ache. Push, push, push. The bulging fish finally pushed so deeply into this crevasse that he came head to head with the end of it and stuck there fast. He had been so busy trying to stop the pain in his stomach that he did not notice that he was in fact pushing himself into the crevasse. Now, however, he was firmly stuck there. He tried moving forward, but the bulging fish was stuck fast. He bubbled out at passing fish but he was so deep in the crevasse that no one could hear him. Panic struck, he realized that he was going to be stuck in this crevasse forever, never to be seen again. He would die here with no one to love him or care for him. Bubbling away to himself, he cried and moaned, moaned and cried. Bubble, bubble, bubble, sniff, sniff, sniff.

Hours went past while the bulging fish bubbled with desperation, until it finally struck him that he had not eaten in that whole time, not one bite. Now he was no longer bubbling and sniffing, he was panting and sweating. No food for bulging fish! No food in more than three hours! Pant, pant, pant, sweat, sweat, sweat, panic, panic, panic! The bulging fish was in a terrible state with no one to hear him in his hour of need except one little fish that swam right by a little hole above the crevasse. She bubbled into the bulging fish asking if he needed any help. In his utter desperation he cried out that he was stuck in this crevasse and was dying of hunger! This darling little fish could not see the whole of the bulging fish through the small hole and so she asked him to hold up his mouth to the hole so that she could give him what he needed. She did all she could to feed this hungry bulging fish but there was only so much she could get through the small hole.

Days passed with the little fish appearing daily to feed the bulging fish. The bulging fish had much time to reflect now that he was spending so much time not eating and he had many questions to ask of the little fish. He loved to hear about her day and those she had met on her travels to and from this small hole. The little fish also brought some of her friends to visit the bulging fish and they took it in turns to feed him.

After one night's particularly restless sleep the bulging fish woke up a little worse for wear. He really had not been comfortable in his usual stuck place as he kept slipping down the crevasse walls. Slipping! It suddenly occurred to him that he was not as stuck as before. He tried to move back out of the crevasse. He moved a little but not enough to free himself fully. He wriggled and jiggled and realized his body was jiggling more than before. He quite enjoyed the movement and started up his own little dance. He began to sing to himself to help the hours pass until the little fish would be back to keep him company and feed his tummy. Jiggle, jiggle, jiggle, wiggle, boom, wiggle. On the wiggle he loved to beat his tail against the sides of the crevasse wall. He enjoyed moving his body to the beat. When the little fish arrived after her day's work he had a new song to sing her and together, with the help of the other fish of the reef, they would sing the chorus. It became quite an affair with more and more fish coming to join the fun.

One night he just could not get comfortable enough to sleep. He lay this way and that, that way and this but he could not stay still long enough to find rest. He began to feel a little sorry for himself all alone in the deep dark of the night, stuck in his crevasse. Moan, groan, moan. However, as he looked up at the hole, the faint glimmer of light passing through reminded him of his new friends above and a song came to his heart and he began to sing. At first he sang quietly so as not to awaken the fish close to the crevasse but as night came to a close and the light of day shone with golden rays across the reef water, his heart gladdened and his voice carried out over the reef.

Waves of joy penetrated the bulging fish's heart as he heard the voices of his friends above join in the chorus, and the rhythm of the music touched every scale of his shiny body so deeply that he started to move with the music. He closed his eyes and felt the music beat within, and his body moved as if commanded by a magician. Swirling, twirling, jiggling, wiggling, bouncing and gliding. The bulging fish was so caught up in the dance that he did not even feel himself glide along through the inside of the crevasse and out into the ocean beyond.

Slipping, sliding, gliding...free.

It was only when he finally opened his eyes that he realized where the dance had carried him; jiggling, wiggling, swirling and twirling.

He was in the centre of a joyful spiral of celebration as his friends swished around him, their bodies moving to the magic of the music he had taught them. He stopped for a moment awe-struck at the beauty of all those friends he had never seen but only heard, and their song echoed through every scale of his body. What a delight to be back in the ocean and to be singing with his new friends.

And there, dancing on the edge of the spiral of fish was the Wise Old Fish, his silvery scales glimmering in the light of delight as his wise old body moved effortlessly in the magic of the moment.

MAKE YOUR CHILDREN STRONG

Make your children strong so that they can shine in this world. Give them confidence so that they know their own strength. Help them to stand up with their heart open. Show them what options are open to them to choose from and allow them to make their choices. Resist the desire to scurry them away from challenges. Give them the flavour of freedom by allowing them to taste it, but reign them in tightly and weave around them a crystal mantle of purity and truth so that they know too what this feels like. Do not be afraid of confrontation. Be afraid rather of lack of communication: it is the greater evil (evil is the reverse of live). You are here together to learn from each other and you can only do that when you are meeting and sharing responsibilities. Do the journey. We are with you in every breath and every heartbeat. We know you know this. Walk in faith.

YOUR PERSONAL POWER

This personal power is tainted by all the limitations that you would place on yourself. You are a pure vessel of love. Now imagine this vessel to be a long thin vase full of clear liquid. Your doubts and fears are like sand and grit and stones that fill the vase and make it overflow, and when it overflows it affects those around, leaving puddles and imprints on their heart.

What you desire is for this liquid to be in its purest state and to be a constant waterfall exchange of pure flowing love. So imagine rather that you are a fountain bowl where there is a constant flow of love and where there is a constant power source illuminating your being, allowing that flow to bring delight to all that witness it. Do not allow your water source to be clogged up with grit and stones. This is what happens when you limit yourself with fears. There is really absolutely no need to fear anyone or anything. You are the pure source of all that is good. The choice to love or to fear is completely your own in every moment of your life; this is free will.

Move from being a vase that believes it is separated from source. Imagine yourself instead to be the fountain that is in continual connection to source and jumps and surges and spills over and splashes with the delight of pure love. Know this to be true and devote yourself to your reconnection to source so that the joyful flow of life fills your every moment of experience.

It is your choice to realize this or your choice to forget. You are loved dearly.

STRIVING FOR MORE

Breathe deep and infuse yourself with the simple knowledge that all is well and in perfect divine order. This is trust; to know that all is happening as it should, and that you are learning, experiencing and feeling for the greatest good of all. When you maintain this belief there can be no room for chaos or panic or worry or fear. So know that all is perfect as it is.

This will not prevent you however from reaching beyond this moment and desiring to achieve more. It is like the baby who is content but reaching forward to copy his brothers and sisters so that he may move to the next stage of movement whether that be crawling or walking. So striving for more is a constant quest because you are here to learn and make the most of every second this existence has to offer. And know that even in the striving there is perfection, so rest easy, even in the striving!

When you hold a yoga pose for example you are resting in the knowledge that all the work, that has got you to this point of expansion and body awareness, is honoured, and you can envision further expansion ahead but you are simultaneously honouring the present moment of where you are. This is balance. It is indeed a fine balance because you do not want to fall backwards or tread water for too long nor do you want to rush ahead chaotically before everything is ready and forget something, or in the case of yoga, do damage to your body.

You want to find the elusive in-between stage, and when you are comfortable here then expansion is yours. It will come to you and, before you know it, you will be in another increment of balance before expansion comes to reclaim you again. It is almost as if you are on a railway line advancing by increments or sleepers. However, you must know that expansion is not only in a forward linear motion for as you advance the whole world advances with you and the vista constantly changes as you move along the track.

It is an orchestra of movement that is so perfectly choreographed that its magnificence would leave you awe-struck. Chug along gracefully and with ease knowing that there is a whole network of woven brilliance surrounding your every advancement. We rejoice in every tiny increment of expansion. Do likewise and enjoy the journey. We are all on the most truly glorious of adventures together.

DANCING WITH LIFE

Sit up straight as we infuse you with your love. Yes, it is your love, the love of you; the love that you have created, the love that all your angels, guides, masters and loved ones breathe into you and mirror to you. It is the dancing swirl of tornadoes of ecstatic love and joy and frivolity.

You have become a little serious; it is such a sickness. Seriousness is one of the greatest ills of your existence because it brings with it the furrowed brow, the worry, the heaviness, the lack of lustre, the lack of joviality, the lack of flow. It is heavy and gooey and we find it more difficult to reach you when you are there.

Why do you become so serious? We know you have so many responsibilities and obligations. You are important and you are out to save the world! How could we forget! You certainly do not. For God's sake, for the sake of the Creator, let go! Come on, you have tried this countless times and it does not work. It just leads you into a spiral of indecision and lethargy.

We love you with all our might but we labour with you when your over-responsibility kicks in. You carry the weight of the world on your shoulders and that is not what you are asked to do. You are asked to live in the joy that is your divine birthright. Sit up straight, lower your shoulders, breathe in, now put on some music and dance. You have not left your computer but already inside you are dancing.

We see the dance and you feel the dance, and it feels good. The breath is deepening and releasing and the cells are jiggling and loving this new vibration. Let it flow, let it flow, let it flow, let it flow.

Move from one activity to another with the fluidity of joy and expectation! Be creative in everything you do, even your boring paper work. As you do, listen to uplifting and upbeat music; something that feeds your soul. Know that you are more than your head. Feed your senses richly when you are doing your 3D work. Spoil your senses with the vibration of music. Do not miss a moment to feed yourself with the loving vibrations of joyful music. We love you so, oh we love you so. Enjoy the rhythm of life in the music you hear. Listen with your heart. Your cells are dancing in the swell of the wave of sound. Surf this wave deep into your soul. Feel it crash with power and feel the rush of extra life energy course your very being.

These waves ride the ocean of your being, through all the systems of life exchange; the exchange of oxygen, the renewal of lymph, the pumping of the blood around your body. Feel the pump and piston action, the rise, crest and fall of the wave, the constant movement, the constant renewal of life, the constant in-breath and out-breath of LIFE. You are a living miracle, how can you not feel impassioned in every moment of your life? You have the love of the Creator that acts as piston, power and life-giver. Enjoy, enjoy, enjoy.

We ask you to turn up the volume on your music, on your passion and on your joy, and allow the healing rhythms of the music to woo, charm, seduce and enliven you. We will dance with you. All life is movement, feel it in the drumbeat and the melody of the voice, the percussion, the undulating sounds. Let it rush through you with vigour and love. We beat out our love for you and join with you in this ecstatic celebration. Peace to you.

STUCK IN A CREVASSE

I am feeling too earthbound and stuck in my ways. I don't feel that I have a way out.

Like the bulging fish you are simply learning that there are moments of being stuck in the crevasse while slowly but surely you are receiving from on high the information you need to download so that you can move into bigger oceans. This is simply the process that is taking place here, so do not worry. You know from experience that everything always works out, so walk in faith.

THE WISDOM OF YOUR CHILDREN

What would you have me know especially with regard to the upbringing of our children?

You have seen in your garden that the bulbs are pushing up through the soil ready to blossom. That is just like your children. What a delight to see them ready to shine in this world. Water them with love, sprinkling them regularly so that they never thirst for it. Shine on them with rays of joyfulness and light so that their hearts remain unburdened and gay. Cherish their failings as their faltering steps will one day lead to confident strides that bring with them a wave of change. These new arrivals on the Earth have much to teach, much to share. If you listen carefully in fact, you will notice that they never stop teaching. They say, "Hey mama, come and play this game," or, "Hey mama, come and dance with me," or, "Hey mama. I am tired; let me sit on your knee!" They know intuitively what it is they need. They are teaching you to nurture your needs. Pay close heed.

Have you noticed how they can hop from one emotion to another without so much as a blink of an eye because they are allowed to express it in its fullness? They do not wrestle with their emotions, they express them. Do likewise, and you will find that you will inhabit your body with greater ease.

The child is the unconscious expression of Spirit made incarnate. Be childlike consciously and your zest for life will return. Do not be afraid. Make little inroads and we will help you along.

When your heart is heavy

When your heart is heavy it sends a signal to your whole metabolism to slow down to a snail's pace. Your natural state of being is one of joy. This can be difficult for you to sustain in the world in which you live but make this your constant quest and you will find yourself feeling uplifted and being inspirational to those around you.

Dare to dream and keep dreaming

With the arrival of spring come hope and warmth and the joy of the new blossoming of life. All the underground work is completed and now it is time to move into the pleasure of experiencing the opening of the petals and the revealing of all your colours. Do not let your petals droop but open them to the sunshine so that they may radiate the beauty of the Creator's light.

Do not hide, for every single flower has a different hue and the spectrum of these coloured lights may only shine in their full majesty if each single flower plays its part. Shine, let it shine, let it shine.

Dare to dream and keep dreaming. That is why you are here. You are here to show that you can dream and that dreams do come true. Do not fool yourself into believing that once you dream one thing then it is carved in stone and unchangeable. Be more malleable in your creations. Create and if you do not like it, recreate. It is that simple, and, what is more, the process is speeding up so that what you do not like can be changed in the shake of a lamb's tail.

Let go of the illusion that you are tied to anything or anyone because that is fear. You are literally as free as a bird. You are the one that places yourself in the cage, and we know this thought frustrates you deeply. So rise above your frustration and spread your wings. You will enjoy the view.

You are advancing into unchartered waters. We watch your every step with bated breath. It may seem such a huge step for you but believe us when we tell you that it is but a tiny step to the top of this particular mountain and then you will enjoy the most beautiful view.

Do not worry that there is a whole range of mountains beyond this one. Each summit brings a pleasure all of its own. This mountain range is in an area of the world yet undiscovered so every step is a whole world of discovery on its own.

Enjoy. Go see what you can create and enjoy.

THE CERTAINTY OF ACTION

You are a sovereign being that holds the key to your own destiny. You are an intimate and intricate part of the free expression of the Creator. Do with it as you *will*. There are no boundaries, there are no rules, there are but the laws of life that govern the outcomes of choices. You will know these laws for they act as the mirrors to choices made.

Everything arises out of a choice between fear and love. It is by experiencing the choices from both sides that you learn to choose what is best as it will ultimately be what *feels* best. So use this as your yardstick and in every moment of your day simply pose yourself the question. Am I undertaking this work or action out of love for myself or out of fear? And if there is uncertainty then know that this is not truly love, and take the time to discover why.

Love is an all-encompassing certainty of action. It is a propulsive certainty that radiates out from the soul quality that surrounds you. It is the feeling of security and belonging that you yearn; the security blanket that you yearn. This is a blanket that radiates out into a universe of cushioned and cradling adventures of the limitless expression of 'All That Is'.

Fear, on the other hand, will turn the mirror inwards and downwards into a spiral of self-loathing, rejection and hardness that will leave you feeling brittle and edgy if this feeling is entertained.

Find love in all you do and you will discover that it brings with it a myriad of potentials and discoveries and illuminations. This is your birthright, this is your 'being', this is your so-called New World; it is the stepping into your multi-patterned blanket of love. You are sovereign. You are love. You are 'All That Is' in the expression of the love that is your totality. Be sovereign unto yourself, embrace what resonates as your own, and release what does not so that it too may find resolution.

JOY IS MY BIRTHRIGHT

I open my heart to the joy that is my birthright.

When you smile and laugh you open the floodgates to inspiration and joy. Smile so that your luscious lips extend to your dainty earlobes. Look at and feel the present of your lips. They taste, they feel, they pout, you lick them, you paint them to make them shine. When you smile you reveal the pearls of your being, and we are not just talking about your polished teeth! The smile radiates out from your inner being, from your desire to move out into the world and share a part of your being with all of the divine beings that surround you.

Your laugh is an explosion of joy into the space that surrounds you. It is an ecstatic and automatic celebration and realization of your divinity that comes rushing out of you when you sense your belonging and when you fall in love with yourself. Allow your laugh to make love with you and feel the release along your spine. Allow your lips to break into the smile of the recognition that you are a divine sensual being. This smile breaks momentarily the longing to belong as it opens you to the sharing with another and the longing to simply `be` in the moment.

You imagine that there is a moment for being spiritual, for being sexual, for being happy, for being silly, for being serious. You can be all things at all times. Children do this so naturally. They delight in their being. They delight in the freedom of running naked, shouting at the tops of their voices until it is frowned upon by the adulterated world. They delight in the sensations of the physical body which feed the emotional, mental and spiritual bodies. Break free from the separation that has been inflicted on these four bodies and allow them to dance freely with one another. Cry when you need to, laugh when you need to and forever feel the freedom and natural sensuousness of your being. It is otherwise known as deep relaxation and inspiration and is the most natural state of your being. Open up to life and allow yourself to feel free.

TRUTH

Truth is the key to the revelation of the essence of who you are. It is something you feel or sense. We talk about the Higher Self and immediately you imagine that Higher Self to be outside of you, above you, beyond you, in Heaven, separated from your earthly existence, whereas when we talk about your essence it is something that we see you recognize as resonating from within you.

If, anatomically, you had to pinpoint this place you would point to somewhere in the belly region or more exactly your solar plexus. Either way there is a physical reaction to your essence that manifests itself in your body, which creates a feeling of expansion, reassurance and love. This is, in essence, your essential self. So trust this resonance within your physical frame. It is a gift from the Creator and an echo that resounds throughout your physical being that allows you to discern your truth. It is the essence of who you are that allows you to be in truth.

ONE WAY ONLY TO SURVIVE

There is only one way to survive, and that is through the trusting of who you are, the essence of who you are. You must know that you are of the light and that the light does not leave you. You merely choose to hide the light sometimes so that you can rediscover it in its magnificence.

You can choose however to be of the light with every breath you take and see what adventures that leads you into. We would wish for you to experience the light of who you are and radiate it out to all those around you. Move out of fear and limitation and embrace the fullness of all that you can be in all moments.

LOVE YOURSELF, AS WE LOVE YOU

We wish only that you could love yourself, as we love you. Let us today weave this love deeply into your physical being. Be attentive all day long to the love that is constantly available to you and swirling around you. Be in love with yourself, your greater self, your whole self and nothing but yourself. Love, love, love is all that there is. Breathe it into your soul with every breath you take and watch the miracle unfold.

NOT AFRAID TO SING

Rest easy in the knowledge, that all is in perfect motion and time. The little bird sits on the branch in the garden and sings out its song for the whole world to hear. It does not bother that its song might wake up the neighbourhood or that it is not the right time for that kind of song or this or that. No, it just sings. And so it is with you, just sing and see what happens.

THE CENTRE OF THE WORLD

Close your eyes and imagine yourself to be in the centre of the world. In the deepest recess of her heart where you are warm, snug and secure. You are in the centre of the universe looking out at creation.

Now imagine that your body is moving from one plane of existence to the other, through the whirling motions of reality.

Are you choosing with every breath the reality that you desire to be part of? It is simple: you can choose to be happy, grumpy, fulfilled, troubled or joyful. The choice is yours. The fears are simply choices of existence. What do you choose for yourself this day? What do you choose for yourself in this lifetime? Do you choose based on others' aspirations for yourself or do you choose what sings to your soul, your mind and your spirit?

IS MOTHER EARTH LABOURING?

The social harmony of the world, as it stands, leaves much to desire. But it is indeed your desire that will see the blossoming of the love and respect of every woman, child and man coming to the fore.

When the winds of change settle and the rains of purification have wet your lands it is time to rise from the mud and shine. There is much releasing, much perturbation as the resistance to change grips at your souls. But the butterfly emerges from its cocoon and the flowers open their petals so that their scent flows on the breeze of lightness and joy and newness. This experience is a first for mankind. We, in the heavenly realms, watch in awe as your creative minds come up with loving solutions to the problems of your existence. We see many brilliant minds and hearts melding into the creativity that is your birthright so that this world may once again flourish and radiate. It may appear for many that Mother Earth is labouring. Indeed in many parts of her body she is paining but she too is releasing as the new comes to her. With every release you make on fears, limitations, set beliefs and habits that no longer serve you, you allow Mother Earth to release part of her pain.

The land is calling you back to her. Her longing is deep. As you walk, each plant, each stone, each tree beckons to your essence. If you walk in awareness you will recognize their call and know that you are one. The universe is a swirling vortex of activity that is mirrored in your individual biology. With each inhalation there is change and with each exhalation release from change and the acceptance of the new. You are a constantly transforming 'being'. It is your choice, with every inhalation, to inspire yourself to renewal or to hold tightly onto what you know to be old and familiar, even though it may feel so uncomfortable to you.

Do not withhold your breath. Breathe deeply and know that, with each inhalation, inspiration flows to you, bringing you to a new place of discovery; a new balance. The inhalation and exhalation make a pair so that what no longer serves you can be released and leave a space that brings you into a new part of the journey.

Why do you think that your breath becomes shallow in times of great stress and anxiety? It is because the fear has gripped you so tightly that you are afraid to move forward. In these moments of fear it is often difficult to remember to breathe in deeply as the fear takes hold, so release deeply with the out-breath and the in-breath will follow like day follows night.

The pain of release can be lightened by engaging with Mother Earth. She is offering gifts daily and yet you hide in your offices, in your buildings, inside, away from her loving touch. Imagine that as you walk along her shore or in the heart of her forests that she is wrapping you with a blanket hewn from a love so pure that it will melt all in your heart that no longer serves you on this journey. She is the greatest healer of all. She is the ultimate mother of all. Every plant, rock, boulder, tree, bush, droplet of water contains within it the magic of 'All That Is' and it is available free of charge. It is an abundant universe that desires to be of service, should you so choose to accept.

Come and play outside beloveds. Don your coats or your cream but come and play. Your birthright is joy and Mother Earth will tickle you with delight.

GOING BEYOND WORDS

To go beyond words, connect to the heart of your communicant as you weave to them, from your own heart, the message you desire to send. In this way you bypass the hold that the mind will want to make on the words chosen and instead the message will reach their heart space. Once there the mind will acquiesce in finding the words necessary to describe the emotion received.

Your heart space resonates with more force, vigour, intent and truth quotient than your mind or ego can ever hold.

LAUGHTER

Enjoy laughing. Laughter is a cure to all ills. It keeps your spirit light and brings simplicity to all situations no matter how heavy and difficult they may feel. Cultivate your sense of humour and in doing so you will find the light-heartedness in all things in your life.

Self-derision is also a tool to use so that you do not fall into the trap of taking yourself too seriously. Many have found the cure to their ills and their country's ills through a healthy dose of laughter.

Happy is he who laughs last!

THE LAST STANDING HUMAN

Imagine that you are the last standing human being on Earth. Imagine around you barren ground, the sky above you heavy with pollution, death, waste and destruction. Imagine that all you loved and possessed seems lost in the ethers of time. You are alone, abandoned, distressed and fatigued. Now imagine that within that broken heart there is left but one tiny shimmer of light and as you perceive this light it glows a little stronger and warmer as you give your attention and awareness to it. Your attention is so given to this light and you are so amazed by its beauty that you are, as yet unaware, that all around you the power of this light is bringing to life the barren landscape that just minutes before you found yourself in. At your feet new life pushes through the ground and is mirrored in the sky as patches of radiant blue reveal themselves and the first rays of sunlight reappear. You raise your head as you hear birds singing and your aloneness disappears.

Know that all is directed, created and illuminated through this heart centre light. You are the orchestrator of your universe. You call to your experience everything that you have so thought to desire, everything that you have so feared to live. From today forth call everything you do through the light at the centre of your being. See every experience weave itself through this light in your heart. And for those experiences that seem born from a thought that escaped this light then simply weave it back into the light of your heart, and life in full will return.

It is this simple.

BUT A BREATH AWAY

The breath is the avenue to living consciously.
It is the highway to your destination.
It clears the path to your very being.

It brings with it the rush of inspiration and newness.
It connects you to the very heartbeat of the earth and the source of all creation.
As you breathe in, you align yourself with the source of 'All That Is'.

"I am alone!" sometimes you cry and yet you are truly never alone for in the sacred bounty of 'All That Is' you are forever linked to the fullness of life through the breath.

Imagine that with every breath you take, you are connecting yourself to the Creator Source, and then my friends your life will change immediately. For with the richness of every breath you can begin to inundate your spirit with this pure connection of life-giving sustenance.

The Creator, in its fullness, breathed life into you so that, in turn, you may live life to the full. This is the secret of life.

Your breath holds for you the secret of *your* life. No one, but yourself, can take this breath for you. You took it at birth and you will release it at death and in between time it is the connection to the source of 'All That Is' and 'All That You Are.' Can you imagine that it is this simple?

You are loved so very dearly, and help and sustenance are but a breath away.

BE CAREFUL WITH YOUR WORDS

Whenever you call my name, I come running.
Whenever you breathe in love, I come singing.
Whenever you bow your head, I come embracing.
Whenever you sing out loud, I come dancing.
Whenever you cry in pain, I come consoling.
Whenever you lose your way, I come searching.
Whenever you feel alone, I come playing.
Whenever you rest in peace, I come rejoicing.

Be careful with your words. They are very powerful and can wound as well as heal. The word carries with it an energetic vibration and each word is cushioned with the energy of the emotion that you are feeling inside. Be very economical with your words. Be like the owl who listens more than speaks, for in his wisdom his words become like jewels in the night.

You have the power, literally, to bring healing with every word you say so imagine that the word that pours from your mouth flows as if from a radiant budding flower. Hold the intention to bring healing and love with your words and they will begin to amaze and heal *you*. Imagine that each word has a consciousness of its own. It is like a child that you are birthing and educating. Do you want this child to be unruly, unkempt and running wildly or would you wish for it to be loving, kind and sweet to behold? Your word is your sword. Sheath it in light. The 's' is for sweetness.

You are never alone. Go lovingly about your day. We are with you always.

THE UNIVERSAL GIFT OF LIFE

It is in the flow of life that one discovers the true richness of the universal gift of life. The synchronicities of life are so interlaced and multifaceted that is too far-fetched not to believe that there is a helping hand.

The reality is that you have a multitude of angelic helpers ready at your beck and call. Ask and you shall receive. Seek and you shall find. You are the master; the master of your creation. If you seek discord and drama then this is what you will find. If you seek peace and calm and expansion and joy then indeed this is what you find. Angelic helpers are at your beck and call but you must do the bidding. So whenever and whatever you command, by law it must be given.

Know your own heart, in which lie your true desires.

MAKE DECISIONS

From our perspective it all seems so simple, so straightforward. We see where you ought to go, where you ought to be, how you could do things differently to make your life flow more easily for you, but in your reality the outplaying of your thoughts needs to happen before you can really see the consequences of your choices. That is why you need to make decisions to help you move forward. Staying put and waiting for life to choose for you is not a way forward. You are simply inviting in stagnation and frustration and then a whole series of depressive thoughts arise leaving you feeling hard done by.

The real and only way to engage fully in your life is to enjoy the process of decision making. Make decisions as this empowers you, and as you feel more empowered you reignite your inner creative power and strength and, as a result, become the ultimate creator of your life's experience.

When you do not make decisions but sit on the fence hoping that things will just sort themselves out you miss out on opportunities to direct the process. Know in your deepest self that you have the power to make the right decision. Ultimately it cannot be anything other than right, for you will know by the experience of your choice whether it is right for you by how you feel, and if it does not feel right then you simply choose again.

This is the beauty of your journey. You are learning by the experience of your choices to choose actively for yourself what it is you desire to experience in your life. And so, as you choose, you experience, and as you experience, you choose, and the wondrous journey of experiencing continues as you refine what it is you desire most. And by choosing to experience what it is you desire most, you begin to experience it.

How do I choose what it is I desire for myself?

What makes your heart sing? Where do you find your voice? Where does the flow happen without effort, without strain? What makes you feel joyous and expansive? Go in search of it because that is what you came to find. This is the elusive gold at the end of the rainbow; the golden dust of passion that comes from the free flow of your energy through the clarity of the rainbow-coloured centres of your being. Trust in your ability to choose for yourself. You have been taught not to trust this inner guidance but it is not for this reason that you have lost the ability.

It is like riding a bike. Get back in the saddle and enjoy the changing scenery again. Ride to the destinations of your heart, your soul and your very being, and watch as your life's journey becomes truly magical. Your heart is the steering wheel, and your intention, the pedals. Watch as the spokes radiate outwards the creation of your life, the one *you* have chosen to live.

ALCHEMY

Alchemy, in its essence,
is the revelation
of the pure essence
of the object of your consideration.
There are so many ways
to look at anything or anyone.
It is the look placed on the object or the person
that brings transformation.
This is your task as an alchemist;
to transform all that you see
and all that you are with
by the loving regard you hold in its favour.
It is that simple.
Beauty is in the eye of the beholder.
Behold all that you see with love.
Purify this look of love
for all that comes into your life.
That is where the mastery lies.

SNOWFLAKE

The snowflake is a multi-patterned miracle of the element of water. It is, however, but a tiny speck in the sky as it falls in a blanket of white upon the earth. And, as it does, this one snowflake melds with billions of others to create a blanket of snow upon your earth. Its intricacy and uniqueness meld into the one blanket that comes to rest upon your land, and all becomes white and bright.

Can you see how truly intricate and unique each one of you, human beings, is upon the Earth? And, in your uniqueness, each of you is contributing to the blanket of love that is descending upon the Earth. This is your singular task, like the snowflake that shimmers in the sky, to bring the unique vibration of your whole being down to the Earth in the flurry of the love of `All That You Are`.

MAKE LOVE YOUR MASTER

Weaving through the cosmic space is a love of infinite refinement and purity. It is sending a shimmer of the most glorious lights to your planet. It weaves incessantly in and out of the layers of energetic light surrounding your planet, bringing a new form of illumination to raise the vibration of your planet from where it vibrates presently.

When you sit in the moment of quiet, that you call meditation, imagine that the fallout from this dense patterning in your light weaves is powdering down onto you in a magnificent ray of warm energy that automatically raises your vibration.

Make love, in all its various forms and expressions, your master.

A FLYING HORSE

Do you remember the story of the flying horse? Every time it returned to land it radiated a brilliant translucence as if it had been beyond the confines of the Earth's limits, although it never had really, and yet this is the point. You are in fact always beyond the Earth's confinement because in reality, you are Spirit. This is your real being. This earthly experience is the opportunity for you to have the joyful experience of being you as a human being.

You are in essence a flying horse. It is for you to use the wings. Do you get it? You think that you are more like a horse in a field and that you cannot fly; you just have to keep trotting around the field eating grass and doing what all other horses do. Perhaps from time to time you might jump a wall here and there or gallop along a trail for the thrill of it. But you do not actually believe you can fly, and therein is the first great lie you have believed.

You are, in fact, a flying horse. Go fly. Spread your wings and reach beyond the confines of who you believe yourself to be. Keep going beyond the belief systems you have. Keep looking behind them to see how much further you can go. Release the wings that are bound to your back.

How?

You will do this by not allowing yourself to be limited by the walls in your field. Keep jumping the walls in your field, and by this we mean that you must constantly and methodically rediscover the fullness of 'All That You Are' by looking beyond the confines of what you believe you are. Always look beyond to 'All That You Are' in essence.

The greatness of 'All That You Are' is all you desire to be. So come back again and again to what it is you desire for yourself; you, the flying horse, desires for itself. And that is freedom of the skies. You do not have to pass beyond the Earth's confinement to attain freedom. Freedom is here and now.

WELLBEING

It is by the simple inhalation of wellbeing that we come to it. How very simple and uncomplicated it is but as a human you tend to enjoy the complication of life, otherwise you fear boredom.

Take away the fear of boredom and fill it with the simple elixir of `being`.

This pressure to do and to achieve is an illusion of grandeur when in fact in your `being` the grandeur is already illuminating your heart and soul.

STAR DANCE

Once upon at time there was a wall of illusion surrounding the castle of your heart. It is now breaking open, and revealing an expanse of land, limitless and expansive, to the view. You are moving beyond the confines of your fears and your hitherto beliefs. This is what we call `living`. Sometimes tears need to be shed for the wall to break and crumble and there are moments of panic at the thought we may be destroying something that protects us, cushioning us within the `known`. But now the open expanse is calling. Fly swiftly towards your dreams.

We have a story to tell…

There was once a man who lived within a forest. His house belonged in a cosy clearing of his own making with the sun penetrating the space around him. He went contentedly about his work gathering wood for his fire, and roots, berries and leaves for his meals. His own company gave him satisfaction and he had no longings. At night he would sit in his rocking chair contemplating the clear expanse of the night sky and the multitude of stars.

Until one night out of the darkest part of the sky shone a star so brightly that it caught his attention. Intrigued he watched it attentively. It began to spin and move forwards and backwards as if approaching and retreating from him in a dance of introduction. There was no fear, just an intense concentration on the man's part. The dance continued with the star leading the man by the tip of his intensity and curiosity until he became quite caught up in its movements; backwards, forwards, sideways, to and fro in an ecstatic joyful dance of meeting and reconciliation.

There were light years between this man and the star but their union was joyful and uncomplicated, intimate and serene. The pipe lay on the ground, the rocking chair rocked its own tune and the man whirled in the fullness of the clearing to the cadence of his soul.

Know that you hold the connection of light years in your soul. You are as large and as wide, as deep and as long, as sparkling and scintillating as the stars in the sky. Claim your majestic brightness and sparkle for your deepest joy. You are deeply loved.

THE ENJOYMENT OF CHOOSING

When the time has come all will become clear about the path you have chosen. The whole point of the journey is the enjoyment of choosing. What is inherently special is that your choosing is always right because it simply leads you into the experience of 'All That You Are'. When your choice does not please you, you can simply complete the experience and choose again. It is vitally important that you do however come to completion in the experience of your choices otherwise they will manifest and re-manifest until the learning is acquired.

The experience must be fully downloaded otherwise it constantly reappears. It is similar to the dialogue boxes that appear on your computer when you have interrupted a download or when it has been interrupted because of some technical incompatibility. The software is programmed to warn you that it has not been able to complete the full process of downloading and that you have not fully downloaded the fullness of the experience that you have chosen for yourself.

So if you want to move on and out of an experience make sure that you are taking the time to fully live the experiences that you have already chosen to be part of your existence and come to the fullest completion that you can within them. You know that you must receive the hundred percent download before the programme will work for you, and so it is with your life. Before you can really put into practice what you preach you need to understand it one hundred percent and that can sometimes take a lifetime.

So rest easy in your learning knowing that it is a process but at the same time remain at all times focussed in experiencing the fullness of the journey that you are actively choosing for yourself, and indeed you will come to completion again and again.

How will I know I have reached completion?

The process of completion is ongoing but you will very easily recognize for yourself the repetition of certain themes in your life, and when you recognize repetition you will know that there is still something to be learned. When you come to this realization then it is time to search for clarity, and to search for clarity you must simply intend for it to be there and the answer will appear. All of this requires for you to be fully present to the life you are leading and the choices you are making.

A PAW FROM HEAVEN

It was so in the beginning that many of your wisest beings would hold themselves in a place so close to Earth that they would be able to see, feel and even touch humans but the reverse was not true.

These beings held a safe space of heavenly energy around certain people and situations with the express aim of infusing life energy and 'wholiness' into situations where the pain of suffering and disease was prevalent. Today it is the same. Many angels incarnate or pass through so quickly that you do not consciously notice their presence and yet they are there close enough for you to touch them. As your cat gently places its paw on your cheek and looks at you lovingly, know that Heaven has touched you.

JOY AND CONTENTMENT

When all is said and done there is no greater satisfaction than the feeling of joy and contentment. That is really the soul food we seek, and for the simple joy and contentment of being, you simply have to breathe in this feeling.

"You mock me now. I am so bored with this earthly existence. It is monotonous and repetitive and I am tired of hearing that that is just the way it is".

We know, you are tired and your vibration is low. Your heart is weary and you are feeling alone.

Take each of these emotions that you are weary of and place them in a balloon. Give each balloon a colour and watch it fly high into the sky. As you gaze upwards you will see birds move in a flock across the sky. They fly through each of your balloons bursting them with their beaks, and as the balloons burst they release a whole shower of golden rain, that falls on your face that you have held up to the sky, as you watched your balloons soar.

This golden rain falls heavily on your skin and it pours down the neck of your shirt and soaks you from head to toe, leaving you feeling refreshed and tingling.

Now shout up to the blue open sky what your wishes are for yourself. Shout them out clearly.

What did we hear you say?

You want joy, you want friendship, you want laughter, you want lightness, you want easiness, you want grace, you want warmth, you want to dance, you want music and you want love, love and more love.

Your heart begins to lift a little at the expectation of change. But let us help set your intention. Imagine in the sky a coloured cloud representing each of these wishes. With great conviction imagine that you are lifting off from the Earth and flying into each of these wishes. As you fly through the clouds they become imbibed into your very being. Fly through joy and feel your soul recognize the feeling. Fly through friendship and laughter and know that they are yours. Fly with the delicious lightness of feeling unfettered and free. Fly with the easiness and grace of the master that you are. Fly with the warm wind in your face as your body dances in the currents of love and music that bathe you from on high.

You are not wholly convinced, but your vibration has changed and so will your reality. Keep releasing your balloons and creating your clouds. Know indeed that all is well and is in order in the universe.

PEACE OF MIND

If ever there was a time for peace of mind, it is now. Peace of mind is the condition you achieve when you allow the trust in 'All That Is' to pervade your soul. What we mean is that you must release all expectations, cares and worries and allow the feeling that all is in perfect order to transfuse your whole being. With every thought and worry that arises from your little self, allow the greatness of your bigger self to say, "Peace now, peace now little one, no need to worry. All is in perfect order and all is well".

Do this as if you were trying to calm the worries of your own child, and you will see that this brings a renewed sense of calm. It is only when you have this peace of mind that you can begin to act in the world.

Do not act while trying to find your peace because your worries will manifest themselves in your reality, unless you lay them to rest. Imagine that it is like trying to climb over a very high brick wall when in fact all the time there is a door knob within the wall that opens a door that you had not seen as you were so busy trying to climb *over* the wall. You had convinced yourself that, yet again, the world was testing you and challenging you. You are busy berating yourself for not having trained harder and been fitter so that you could scale this high wall, when all the time if you had simply been at peace you would have noticed the doorknob in the wall revealing the doorway through. These are among the illusions of your time that great 'efforting' is needed.

Peace of mind and peace of heart are the tools that will help you move through any walls blocking your path. Return always and incessantly to the peace within and the doorknobs will reveal themselves.

BE AT PEACE

You are moving now towards a time when heaven and earth are becoming as one and melding into the greatness of 'All That Is'. You are coming to the realization that you are whole, true and sovereign beings onto yourselves. This process can be difficult and tortuous because you are scared to move forward but if you could simply trust in the process then all will be revealed with ease, grace, beauty and poetry. All is truly well, so deeply perfect in its outpouring and outstretching. Be at peace.

THE GREAT HOMECOMING

I feel the tornadoes of change within. Help me to find a place of refuge.

All those that listen to our voice, we honour you so deeply for the changes you are going through and we urge you to hold steadfast as much beauty is in store.

This is not an idle carrot routine for the stubborn mule that does not wish to put one hoof in front of the other. This is the clarion call that you have been awaiting, asking you to step into and remember the fullness of 'All That You Are'; the 'God Self', the 'Sovereign Self'. It is the culmination of lifetimes of experiences and journeys in the experiencing of 'All That You Are'. Reassembling and reintegrating now are all those thousand-fold facets of yourselves that have been out to explore and experience.

Like an army of courageous huntsmen, you reassemble your strength, your wisdom, your learning back into one united force. You are the thousand-fold petals of the lotus back to flower as one.

You have sent out the call and they are returning but sometimes the hardest part is waiting for the stragglers; the last ones to arrive. Be patient until all the huntsmen have returned, and as they arrive greet them with gratitude and love for the journey they have been on for, each one, no matter how scruffy or unsightly they may look, each one had the courage to leave you and seek its own way. And each one has found its way back to you, so welcome them well. Fear not, you will recognize what is your own. This is the Great Homecoming.

SURFING THE BIG WAVES

How do surfers surf the really big waves and what is the connection to yoga and the energy of the wave?

The form of the wave is cylindrical. It reaches upwards to the heavens, curves at its apex and rejoins all that it comes from, as do you in any form of activity. You reach for the apex, hold for a while, meld into the new energy and integrate it; you are just not necessarily aware of it.

On the wave of breath your system reaches up for new life, takes it in, there is a momentary pause and then the new air is integrated into the body. The wave brings new life. It brings transformation. It brings regularity although this may be disturbed by external conditions. As the breath can be disturbed by emotional or physical traumas so too can the waves on the sea be disturbed by the change of wind or a movement of earth.

These beings that are riding the waves; they are literally on the edge of creation. They are on the crest of the wave, a wave of change that is sweeping the Earth and they are saying, "We can ride this one".

EVERYTHING MUST BE BIRTHED

Everything must be birthed and so it is with all that comes into being, it is birthed, whether that be the birth of a star, of a human, of a cell, of an experience, of an emotion, of a hurricane, of a breeze, of a song, of a tear, of a river, of an ocean.

Now what is that energy that births? What is that energy that decides that something must come into being? And what is that energy that brings the desire to fruition and manifests what was not before?

We tell you that there is no such thing as birthing from anew. The birth of something is the awakening of *your* perception of it. It is the coming of it into your reality, into your everyday three-dimensional reality. For in truth there is no beginning, there is no end, there is only the continuation of 'All That Is' and the recreation and re-expression of 'All That Is'. The real magic is in the infinitesimal forms that this expression of 'All That Is' can take. And that is why you are all part of the One, expressing itself. Each one of you is a form of this almighty expression of 'All That Is'. Do you see?

We return you to the metaphor that we have used before; a blanket of snow is made up of countless intricate expressions called snowflakes that express the appearance of snow upon your lands.

And you, how much more intricate and complex are you in your infinitesimal expressions of what you term God. You are this God; a blanket of love. For no matter how hard you try you cannot get away from the expression of this love that is God. Even when you feel 'out of love' and distanced from it, the yearning to return to love is so great that you almost extinguish yourselves in the search for it. But no matter how long or how far you search, this love of God *is* you. You only distance yourself from it so that you can rediscover it and remember that you are the deeply intricate snowflake of love that is the blanket of 'All That Is'.

Now is the time in your evolution to remember the role you play in this blanket of love. Imagine yourselves weaving through the holes in the snowflakes filling them with the elixir of the love of 'All That Is'. Allow the snowflakes to fall in a blanket of love that encompasses this globe, and weave your heartfelt love and compassion through everything that you do and say. This is your soul task. This is all, ultimately, that you ask or will ever ask of yourself, no matter where you are or what you are doing. Fill in even the holes in the snowflakes with a love that will weave a blanket of love around this world that is you.

LISTEN TO YOURSELF

Your frustration with yourself is tangible as you are reaching the stage now where you know it is not for you to watch the goings-on of others or search for their approval.

You are Spirit unto yourself and your inspiration is to come directly from your Self. You need to spend time connecting with your purpose and give your attention to that in your daily life.

This is your calling….reply or hang up… it is up to you but do not listen into others' conversations.

FEELING WOBBLY INSIDE

When the winds blow through the centre of your universe dislodging all that teeters in readiness to fall, then you will feel all wobbly inside too.

At these shifting times you need to show much compassion for yourself and understanding for the process that is unfolding within. You will see that your life will so arrange itself that you will be able to give yourself the time to rest and nurture yourself more. It is simply your task to look out for the symptoms.

You may feel teary or upset for what seems no good reason or desperately tired and weary of life. These are signs to ask you to release any burdens you are carrying and to stretch yourself out for a rest.

Do not worry that 'things' will not get done, the universe is forever providing for you. You simply need to recognize this law of supply and you will be forever provided for. When you ignore the signs you are headed for struggle and discomfort, and the struggle and discomfort will simply increase until you can no longer bear it and, hey presto, you are made to lie low through a sickness or whatever other physical manifestation so that Spirit can continue with the process of dislodgement within. This dislodgement is simply an inner spring cleaning.

Imagine if you did not continually clear and clean your home and work space, very soon it would be difficult to circulate around your house, and you would have increased difficulty finding what you need at the time you need it. So it is with your inner home, it needs a spring cleaning of all the thoughts or belief systems that no longer serve it.

THE FEAR OF FAILURE

How do I cross the fear of failure?

Like a bridge; you can either, jump across, hop across, skip across, crawl across, or slither across holding on to both sides in case you fall. The choice is always yours. It is intrinsically yours to choose, and in doing so you will create your journey.

Make the intention to cross the bridge in the style you choose, and so it will be. As you falter in the middle of the bridge or take a few minutes to look down at the almighty drop wondering what it would be like to crash upon the rocks below or how it would be to be swept in the raging torrent of the fast moving water then fear may re-enter your heart and you might be tempted to run back. But if you look carefully you will see that you have already gone half the way and to go back would be as challenging as it would be to go forwards at this stage. So in many ways your choice has been made.

Unless, of course, you begin to fear what lies beyond the bridge; maybe somebody is going to jump out and grab you once you have crossed the bridge, or somebody is going to tell you that you are trespassing and should not be there, or maybe the bridge is weaker at that part of the bridge and may crumble under your weight. What other catastrophic scenarios can you dream up? Yes indeed, the realization of any of these scenarios would make you want to flee!

Now, take a breath and imagine and feel how wonderful it would be to cross this bridge skipping along. Take time to stop and watch the smooth flow of the river beneath you. Take time to sit and relax for a while on this bridge knowing that it is strong and resistant and has supported many ones passing from one meadow to another. Have a picnic on the bridge. Know that there is no hurry! And know that certainly on the other side is the most wonderful vista to be discovered.

When you face challenges in your life know that they are simply acting as bridges to a new reality, a new meadow of existence where the grass *will* be greener. Always use a challenge as a bridge to a newer place and know that the universe in its benevolence will always hold you high out of the swirling and dangerous whirlpools of the river below.

You are forever safe.

FACETS OF THE ONE UNIVERSE

For now the pendulum is swinging without wavering. You are at the centre of the universe of yourself and moving with speed towards the realization of `All That You Are`. The time is now for the fruit is ripe for the harvest. There is no need to live in any other moment than the one that you currently find yourself in. This is the sacred moment of being. When you come fully into the now moment you embrace `All That You Are`. There is no greater gift that you can give yourself or humanity for, as you see, humanity is yourself. You are all facets of the one universe, an ocean of `beingness`, an ocean of undulating waves flowing onto the shore of redemption and completion.

The tide is rising, the moon is high and the stars light your way. Allow your being to not only feel the waves but to be the waves as they come crashing into the shore of the awakening consciousness. Feel the forward motion but know that the wave will turn in on itself and return to the wholeness of the ocean to find re-expression of its oneness as it again crashes on the shore of this new consciousness.

We are at a time of evolution that has hitherto been unseen as indeed every moment in the past was a new creation in time and space. You are walking a new path as you do in every moment. The sacredness of this path is created through the conscious awareness on your part of the role you play in its creation. It is indeed all choice and your choice will have a bearing on the shore of the conscious awakening. Feel the energy of these words.

LIFT THE VEIL

The time has come to lift the veil on your heart.

Breathe in the feeling of forgetfulness and feel the haze of memory loss surround you like a blanket that covers your eyes, heart, head and senses. Feel yourself buried beneath this blanket that has closed you to the world beyond and to the fullness of yourself.

Imagine now that this blanket leaves a little slit through which shines the piercing light of day. At first the light stings your eyes and overpowers your senses leaving you feeling a little dazzled, as you are so used to being cocooned within the darkness of your small blanketed world. The light is so bright that you cannot help but move to initially close the slit to find the warmth and comfort of your dark but familiar space.

Something has changed however and this blanketed space is no longer quite the same. Your attention moves to the slit and your desire to see behind the blanket. At first you open it gently so that your blinded eyes can grow accustomed to the new light. You pull it back even further, amazed at what you discover behind it. As you continue to pull back the blanket you grow all the more amazed and overcome by what lies behind until very soon the blanket becomes a cumbersome object that you feel more inclined to set down completely. Now you welcome the warmth and brightness of the whole spectrum of light as it caresses your skin and bathes your senses.

And so it is, as you awaken to yourself. You are simply learning to lift the veil; the blanket of what feels like comfort, to reveal all that you search. Know that you are moving towards the warmth and light; an almighty vastness that will surround your being and cover you and enlighten you more than the blanket that can only offer limited warmth and comfort. The vastness of your being is the illumination you seek. Enjoy the unveiling of your Self and revel in the infinite beauty of you.

In all things look for that slit in the blanket that brings the light home.

YOUR HIGHER OFFICE

And so it is, and so it is indeed that we are among you and with you and of you, for as we breathe in your essence we mingle with you and come to a place of love and understanding with you. We see you sitting in your office surrounded by your books and your files and your full in-tray of 'things to do', and we feel you tighten a little at the knowledge of what you call your awaiting administrative business. And we are here to help.

Yes indeed as you more fully integrate your Spiritual Office we come more fully to understand your human obligations or shall we call them your limitations? To be obliged to anyone or anything creates a circle of vicious tail-following. Have you ever seen a kitten or a puppy run after its tail only to fall into a heap of total exhaustion as it realizes it is never going to get it? And so it is with any obligation you undertake, you are never going to get to bury it. For even as you believe you bury it, the circle of life is already recreating it in a different form.

So how do you stop what feels like an endless tail-following circle of obligations? We would suggest that you sit in them for a while and imagine yourself in a Jacuzzi. Let it bubble around you, sink into it until you begin to feel all warm inside. Now if you have ever sat inside one of those bubbling Jacuzzis you will have noticed that there is a point of discomfort as you first get in. It can feel just a tad too hot or too bubbly until you find your seat and then you really get down into it and begin to enjoy the soothing heat around your limbs. The bubbles rise and bring pleasure and warmth to your aches and pains and you begin to let go a little until the pleasure almost becomes too much to bear and you begin to feel yourself ready to jump out and do something else; the intensity of the heat and bubbles has had its full effect, and enough is enough.

The problem with your obligations is that you do not heed the feeling of 'enough is enough' because you feel this inner compulsion or fear to forever keep going after what it is you think you need to be going after, which is probably: income, a feeling of owing something to others, a fear of being perceived lazy or inefficient! This is what leaves you like that helpless puppy following that blasted tail that you are never going to catch.

And so we would say, with great honour, indeed for all that you do create and make happen, sit in the Jacuzzi only for as long as you feel good in there, and when you are ready to jump out and dry yourself, do that very thing. There is no one in a better position than you to tell you when it is time to get out. Imagine indeed if someone was standing by the Jacuzzi with a stopwatch. Do you think you would really feel at ease to sink right down into it at your leisure if that were the case? And so it is with all that you undertake, sit there only for as long as it feels comfortable.

Avoid separating your life into categories; work, play, meditation, and allotting time to each one. Go with the flow of what it is your desire calls you to in the moment and you will see that all will come to fruition as your desire so wills it. And you will be a happy puppy that has finally discovered that to run after your tail might enthrall you for a moment or two but inevitably will lead you to lying puffed out on the floor with your head in a bit of a spin.

We so delight to be of service to you in all that you do. We are with you, of you and about you at all moments.

Your Higher Office.

THE FREEDOM TO CHOOSE

If everything was really as perfect as you so desire you would find it difficult to create. You have, by virtue of your choice to be human, decided to experience the contrasts in what you desire and do not desire, so that you may exercise the freedom of choice. So do not feel curtailed or limited in the fact that all is not as you wish, for if it were you would lose the freedom to choose.

LIGHTNESS OF BEING

Lightness of being is a habit that can become quite addictive if you let it. As you practise lightening your thoughts you are embracing enlightenment. To lighten your thoughts think *only* thoughts that are supportive and loving of you and all those close to you. When you experience feelings of heaviness and dread know that your emotional body is trying to bring light or attention to your thoughts. So embrace your emotions and states of being as indicators of how well you are doing at allowing truth to be your guide. You will know when your thoughts are in tune with your enlightened self by the feeling of joy and security and happiness that you will feel. All is truly well.

NO LONGER HELD TO RANSOM

The clamour of anger resounds deep from within the belly of the beast and with it roars forth the bellows of fire and smoke destroying what is to die, allowing for new growth. The time of change is upon you. Breathe deep and fire the flame, so that all that is no longer to stay will not.

No longer must you be held in the chains of limitation and dishonour of your being. Roar like you have never roared before and express freely all that divine sacredness of being that will no longer be held to ransom.

A WALK IN THE PARK

Walking in the park is such a leisurely occupation if you have no particular time to be home or no set agenda in mind. This is the trick to living life in joy; walk it like a walk in the park without agenda or time limitation so that you are able to be conscious of what, otherwise, you might miss. You have heard the statement `it was a walk in the park`. In other words, it was something that was easy and unstrained and pleasurable. And so should be your life! All things will come to you when the time is right and in the meantime, enjoy the walk.

DOUBT AND SECOND-GUESSING

There are times, so many times, when doubt and second-guessing are your par for the course, and then you wonder why it takes so many strikes to get the ball to the hole. And that is why you find yourself knocking the ball out of the rough, or chipping it out of the sand bunker.

Once you have teed-off you fully expect the golf ball not to second-guess *its* trajectory. Can you imagine if it did during its free fall through the air, heading this way and that? Your whole game of golf would become a game of chance.

And so it is with you. Why do you second-guess yourself in your assured trajectory towards the whole of what it is you desire? Maybe you like the sand? Maybe you like the rough? Maybe you do. Maybe though you would prefer to hit within par or even better get the hole-in-one?

Keep that hole-in-one or that whole-in-one in mind at all times and know that the impact of your desire will always get you to where you want to be. Be at peace, knowing that all is well.

THE SAFE SPACE

So many times you are at the brink of inspired action when you end up pulling yourself back believing that you are imagining the inspiration. You dive into doubt and second-guessing when in fact the universe's laws had set up the perfect scenario for the realization of your desires.

We do not say this to make you feel bad, quite the contrary. We want you to know that the universe has responded to your every desire, it is simply your lack of security and your feelings of fear that have held that away from you.

And so the solution is easy. Keep working at resolving the fears. The most effective way of doing this is to simply feel safe. Find the safe space and hold yourself lovingly there. Do not do anything that would negatively affect this safe space. You know that this safe space is a space that you create from within, not from without. You know that you simply must feel safe, no matter where you are or what you perceive. Have a 'Keeping Safe Policy' for yourself first and foremost. Keep yourself in that safe space and all that you desire will flow to you effortlessly. It is our promise. Enjoy the unfolding of this promise.

How do I cultivate this safe space? What is your policy on keeping safe?

The breath is the avenue to wellbeing. Take the conscious breath and allow the source of pure energy to invade your body. Do this until you are aware of blocks or of patterns of thought or of any discomfort that comes to your attention. When these pockets of non free-flow present themselves greet them as you would greet an acquaintance. Begin to feel into them and allow your breath to expand so that it engulfs this acquaintance in its embrace. You could compare it to the warm greeting you would give to an acquaintance you have not seen for a long time.

Allow this perceived block in the energy pathway of your being to tell its story while you give it your total, undivided and non-judgemental attention. Just be aware. Let it talk. Let it express. Let it tell its story until you have heard enough and feel that you need to move on then simply say that it was lovely to be with it and you really enjoyed connecting again but that you really need to get back to your work, and wish it a safe onward journey.

As you do this with blockages that come up you will begin to find that they will no longer be there. As you learn to greet them as simple acquaintances you will be able to take a back seat and not identify them as yourself. They are simply aspects of yourself that have served you well. So greet them in this light but do not become attached to them. Let them go on telling their story, and you go on and tell your story, which of course is one of increased wellbeing, happiness and contentment.

When you identify with these blockages then they become as if they are your own and they become attached to you. Allow them their own identity. They simply came to tell you a story. Listen to the story; take from it only what you desire and only what serves you to make your story the one *you* desire to follow.

BE YOUR OWN SUNSHINE

All summer long we yearn for the sun which does not come and all winter long we yearn for the summer heat. So why do we spend so much time yearning for what does not appear?

There are so many ways to live. You can live trusting that all is well as it is or you can live complaining that it is not as you would wish it to be.

Which attitude gives you the most relief? Just knowing that all is well as it is or that something is wrong?

You could just decide that all is really as it should be, and you could get your raincoat on, buy yourself an umbrella and boots and get your face wet.

It does no good at all to complain because that just brings everybody down and as everybody goes down worse things happen which accentuates the spiralling downward. So cheer up and get out and enjoy it all. Enjoy the fact that you do not know from one day to the next what sort of day it is going to be and very soon you will begin to enjoy even the rain.

Your real yearning is for the happiness and contentment that the sun brings. So bring that to your experience and the sun will shine on you from within. Be your own sunshine!

FIRING UP THE PILOT LIGHT

It is only when you really let go that source energy can take over. This letting go is done out of complete trust for 'All That You Are' and 'All That Is'. You have been severed from this lifeline of trust through fears and phobias and bad experiences. But even through the bad experiences you somehow knew you would be alright, even at your lowest point there was a glimmer of hope. That glimmer of hope is the pilot light in your gas heater. It stays on all the time and when you turn on your hot tap expecting hot water, the boiler responds by firing up and heating the water that pours through it.

Your soul, your essence, your God, your Spirit is the pilot light that fires up to pour source energy through your experience whenever you make the request for it to do so. If you do not ask, the pilot light will always stay lit but it will have no need to fire up and heat the water or pour light on your situation. Keep asking, through your appreciation of all that you have, for this source energy to fire you up and warm you up. This source of energy and warmth will bring you all the joy, fulfilment and comfort you desire.

HELP ME TO SERVE

To really truly serve, you need to bring yourself to full awareness at every moment you can. Watch the interplay of emotions, the ties that pull at you this way and that, the fears that rear their head with menace as if to endanger your very life. Watch this playing out of beliefs and aspects of yourself and check to see the emotional response they create within you.

Do they create the feeling of wanting to run away from or run to? If the emotion leaves you cross, impatient and frustrated then sit with it and feel it as intensely as you can. Do not fear to feel it in its entirety. Do not analyze it or ask from where it comes. Do not tally with it but do embrace it fully by bringing it completely into your body, right down into your fingers and toes.

It is not looking to you for questions or analysis but for complete acceptance. If you do this, with awareness, you will find the upsetting nature of the emotion evaporate into the recesses of your own vastness.

You can and should do this likewise with those feelings that leave you feeling contented, euphoric, fulfilled. Feel them in their entirety and they will serve to strengthen your connection to 'All That Is'.

Whatever it is that you do, be fully present, and the present of that moment will return to you in full.

To be consciously present in this earthly existence is a gift beyond compare and to hold, preciously and appreciatively, every moment of this existence in your conscience awareness, is to live fully and joyfully. Be always of good cheer and allow this good cheer to create miracles for you.

TO LOVE THYSELF

You cannot give what you have not received but equally, you cannot receive what you have not already given to yourself.

ARE YOU READY FOR CHANGE?

The time has come in which the pendulum of change is swinging at such a rhythm that humanity is getting the opportunity to jump on the bandwagon, as such.

Imagine a train that has slowed down sufficiently for you to jump on. You are going to have to run a little to jump onto this train but that is the commitment and intention you are being called to show.

This train is not going to come into the station and slow down to a stop so that you can lug your baggage on and take your seat. This train has left already and the forward momentum is such that you have to run along the track a little and catch on and jump in.

You are going to want to travel lightly to be able to do that but once you jump up you can be sure someone will hoist you up further by the arm and help you in, just like somebody else did for them. This is a kindly train but it is a-moving. It just cannot stop now and hang around.

This train is the train of change and momentum that you are currently experiencing. The call for change from humanity has been so forceful and intentional that you have now got to really pick yourselves up to stay with the changes that you have called in. It is the time now for you to be the change you want to see.

What are the changes you wish to see?

You desire to live in a beautiful environment.

- It is time then to clean up your back garden and make it beautiful.

You desire to live in a world where people are kindly and patient.

- Be patient and kindly with the people and animals in your household.

You desire to feel abundant and unworried about your finances.

- Appreciate every penny that comes through your door and consciously and carefully spread your pennies into and around your community. Be the flow. Get into the flow.

You desire peace of mind.

- Take the time to empty your mind of thoughts that do not befit the master you are becoming.

You desire a body that is fit and well.

- Treat it like your greatest and most beautiful ally. Feed it when it is hungry. Give it lots of water so that it does not have to scream out to you when it is too late. Anticipate and respect all its needs and do not ask too much of it. Nurture it instead and it will open to you like a flower.

The change that you desire to see can only come from within you. You have been hoping and praying for so long that the change would come from around you and all would be miraculously well. That change is here, move with it.

YOU ARE THE GOD THAT YOU HAVE BEEN LOOKING FOR

After a very deep, rejuvenating and healing sleep I awoke to the words,

You are the God that you have been looking for.

We give you these words as conclusion to the odyssey of discovery this journal has been. You are finally and gloriously coming to the realization that you are indeed this God that you have been seeking. You have searched high and low in sorrow, grief, pain and ecstasy and all along it is the journey through these lands of emotion that have brought you to the greatest of realizations.

You are all that you seek. You are all that you need.

Now spend the rest of your life living according to this tenet. Be the God that you desire to be loved by, be the God that answers all your prayers, be the God that listens and heals, be the God you call out to. Be the God that brings you `luck`, be the God in whom you delight and have faith and trust. Be the God that you pray to, and indeed heaven will be yours and Thy Kingdom will come.

We have so enjoyed every moment of this sharing with you. We delight in all that you are and all that you are becoming. Our joy is great to see you return home to the knowledge that you are all that you need.

The journey has been arduous but along every step of the way we have been with you. As you cried in loneliness we held your hand. As you shouted out in joy, we raised our spirits with you. As you doubted yourself, we could see only your glory.

And now that you are home we embrace you and wait with bated breath to watch the unfolding of the God that you are.

THE GOD THAT YOU ARE

You say, "The God that you are." Can you rephrase that please? It cannot be just me, what else is there…

You are the trinity of expression that allows for the God that you are. If it were to be just the `you` that you know here it would be rather one dimensional, would it not?

You are the God that you are because you are integrating your Higher Office. You are integrating fully the God Self, the Whole of You, the `Wholiness` of you. You are coming into alignment and harmony with the many facets of yourself. You are beginning to trust yourself and follow your will rather than look outside yourself for the answers.

No one can give you the answers you seek for you are the one that must find your answers. You are this glorious piece of the puzzle, and without the realization of the fullness of you the puzzle remains incomplete.

Your mission is not to `miss` one little `ion` of the journey in coming to full completion of all that you desire to create, and to see, and to experience here and now.

Part Two

I really thought that I had been given all the secrets to life through part one of these writings and that my task was to live happily according to them for the rest of my life. I thought this was the end of the book.

Little did I know of the journey that I was about to undertake, with the illness of my son, and how these words would so deeply frustrate me as well as inspire me. It was obviously not enough to hear these words and understand them on an intellectual level I was required to discover and understand them in every cell of my being. I am amazed now when I read part one, as the teachings were such preparation for what was to come.

It was six months after I wrote the last chapter you have just read, `The God that you are`, that Toby, my youngest son, was diagnosed with brain cancer.

It took me another year of trying to survive life, post Toby`s diagnosis, before I was ready to channel again.

ALLOW THE COMMON GOOD TO PREVAIL

Dear Spirit, I felt the calling to speak with you this evening. My heart is low and I have cast a shadow over the relationship with my husband.

All over the land there is a new awakening but it comes like the rumbles of seismic activity within the earth's crust. It rumbles from afar and its effects are felt somewhere much further away and so it is with matters of the heart. Often it is not what appears to be wrong that really is the crux of the problem at all. More often than not the problem is not a problem at all; it is simply the working out of frustrations and belief systems that no longer serve the common good.

When we speak of the common good we liken it to the relationship that is shared in a family context. It is an element that exists by itself and of itself. It is a good that exists above and beyond the family, protecting its identity and its existence. Together you have come to work on common ideals or challenges that limit you and so together you challenge each other to break down all that hinders you from being the limitless human spirits that you are working to become in this earthly existence. And so the pushing of each others' buttons is a strong indication that you are in a period of expansion, a moving out of limiting belief structures that keep you hemmed in and unable to move freely and without resistance.

Allow the 'good', the common good to prevail and harmony will return and all will be well. Allow Spirit to flood the common good and seek not to fix anything in your mind. Just allow Spirit to resolve the resistance.

Why is it that nothing feels like it is working for us at the moment? I feel hemmed in and limited and while I watch others revelling in their lives and enjoying themselves I wonder what I am doing wrong.

Every life has a series of cycles and you are simply in a cycle that requires you to be at home and at the beck and call of your youngest son. This circle will all too soon be completed and you will look back knowing that you gave of your very best at this special time. Neither life nor time is linear. They are circular in movement and intention, spiralling upwards in new levels of discovery and delight and learning and expansion. Remind yourself constantly that all is well and rest easy in this knowledge.

THE EYE OF THE STORM

Whenever the wind blows it does so in circular motion moving from the top to the bottom, whipping up the objects at the base of the spiral. And so it is with your life: the wind blows through the universe of your being, shipping up your objections to test whether they drop in the middle or remain in the centrifugal power scope of the wind spiral.

This tunnelling of existence allows you to remain calmly within the eye of the storm, watching the reality of your life spin around you. The further you advance, the faster the spiral motion, the stronger the centrifugal force. If you spin outside with your objections you become dizzy and unsteady. Like a puppy following its tail, you end up sick and tired. Stay instead in the middle of the spiralling motion, in the eye of the storm, and simply know that the world is turning about you. Let it turn, and you will notice it slow down, and disturb you less, revealing that where you are, is quiet and undisturbed.

THE PRESENT THAT IS YOU

When you sense our call know that it is your Higher Self calling. The calling is a merging into being. That is why you are beginning to feel this overpowering energy of a joy that is tangible, inextinguishable and a constant presence akin to the energy you felt as a child where all is possible and all is in the here and now and yet simultaneously calling to all that is to come. What a delightful way to live, in the joyful expectation of all that is and is to come. No fear or dread or sense of oncoming doom or pain because you know that no matter what comes it is for your good and the good of all.

Our dear beings present on Earth, present yourself with the present that is you. Unwrap with joyful expectation the present of you. Delight in the discovery of 'All That Is' contained in the beautifully wrapped present that is you. Rip yourself open with abandon and then piece yourself together again so that you can fully enjoy the completion of the gift that you are to yourself and the world.

`TO DO` LISTS

The need for speed in the 'doing' of your tasks is the ingredient that brings stress, overwhelm and disorder to your psyche. Rest simply in the knowledge that all will be done at the right time and in the right way and so it will be. It really is that simple but you like to think it needs to be more complicated or difficult. If you could get out of your own way it would all just organize itself beautifully with minimal effort on your behalf. Relax literally in the knowledge that all is in perfect order already and so it will be. Can you let go of this noose around your neck that you like to tighten every so often for maximum effect? Let the noose loose and watch what happens. Things will get done. Why be so hard on yourself? Trust that what you feel like doing, in the moment that you are doing it, is right. Trust yourself.

Fatigue is the result of overwhelm and the doubting of yourself. There is nothing more tiring than questioning yourself and doubting your instinct. The flow occurs when you trust your instinct. You are not lazy so do not fear that you will lie down and never do another thing. This will not happen. You are too progressive for such an act of defiance.

Enjoy the dance, the constant movement, the flow and the progression forward, and do not subject it to a linear timeline. Allow your life to move in concentric circles of expansion and contraction. The breath force that keeps your body alive and ticking does this of its own. If you were to hold your breath many parts of your organism would suffer and atrophy. The same happens in all other aspects of your life. Allow the natural rhythms of contraction, expansion, inactivity and activity, busyness and stillness to fully oxygenate all aspects of your existence.

Do not interfere with progression that knows its own rhythm. Breathe deeply and trust that all parts of your life will be fully oxygenated by the incoming and outgoing rhythms of life.

When you are tired, rest. When you are activated, make the best of this propulsion to make good your tasks.

Respect yourself and all will be well.

WHEN THE GOING GETS TOUGH, YOU GET TOUGHER

When you ride your bike with the wind in your hair and the strength of its force pushing against you, you push harder on the pedals to advance and, in doing so, you gain strength. And so it is in life when the going gets tough you get tougher. You become wiser, more resilient and more capable of discerning what is good and true for you and those you love.

If life were easy the learning curve would be less defined, less intense or rapid. You do not want it to be too easy, you have too much to accomplish this time around. So be easy on yourself and do not fear that you have somehow merited this bad luck or hard times. You have called to yourself much learning, and so the wind has simply blown harder. It has blown out the cobwebs from your being and freshened up the look on your face.

BE FAITHFUL TO YOURSELF

It is safe to talk, to fully express yourself, to be the person you really want to be. This is, in fact, a requisite for living in integrity with who you are. Be faithful to yourself in this pursuit. Constantly challenge yourself to honour your deepest desires, your deepest wishes. Keep that inner dialogue with yourself and pay close attention to the voice within, which is often the quieter voice that asks for more time, more space and more freedom to be.

The rush mindset is a figment of your imagination. Everything is in perfect order and time. Your sense of rush and panic and fear, of not fulfilling expectations, is what speeds up time even more. If you can honour the inner pendulum of motion and desire and fulfilment then everything outside you will regulate itself according to the rhythm of your inner pendulum. Have trust that you can do this. Start to deeply trust this inner rhythm.

WHAT IS MY LIFE PURPOSE?

It is your life purpose to be all that you can be and discover it through the various experiences you call to you. You are living your life purpose, you do not need to go and find it. Whatever you are doing is your life purpose, it is that simple.

Be deeply grateful for all that you are. That is your life purpose.
Be deeply grateful that life flows through your veins allowing you to experience it.
Be deeply grateful that you know what love is and what it is not.
Be deeply grateful that this planet exists so that you can come to the rediscovery of what you are and what you choose not to be.
Be deeply grateful that you get to create and recreate, make mistakes and in doing so make discoveries.
Be deeply grateful that you have chosen to be here now.
Be deeply grateful that you are making this journey with all those around you.
Be deeply grateful that you are who you are for that is your vision piece, your tool for experience, your means to an end, your chariot and your ticket to adventure.
Be deeply grateful that you have the choice to make this experience as deep and as wide as you choose.
Be deeply grateful that you are safe, for you are eternal and there is no right or wrong.
Be deeply grateful that you are a child of God, a piece of the eternal fabric of the universe.
Be deeply grateful that all is perfect as it is.
And so it is.

Do not take this all so seriously. By simply being here you are fulfilling your life's purpose. Be content with this.

YOU KEEP US AWAY

Just feel our love for you. Breathe it in. These feelings of frustration and sadness you have been feeling are your longing for the awareness of our presence. You keep us away by your incessant feelings of obligation and 'to do lists'. Be at peace knowing that everything is working out perfectly. It is ok for you to sit and be still, or to lie down and rest your body. Be easy on yourself, be easy. Really and truly everything is perfectly in order and under control! Just allow us to work with you and through you. Allow us to inhabit you and play with you. Allow us to be enough without you having to work at being better in any way, shape or form. All is well.

THE MYSTERIES OF LIFE

You speak of the mysteries of life and many of you spend a lifetime or more trying to figure them out.

The mystery is, in fact, that you do not recognize and fully acknowledge the piece of the puzzle that you are.

Others cannot be that piece of the puzzle for you. You must come to look at yourself as that piece of the God puzzle that will bring all mysteries to full clarity.

And it is the 'you' that you are right in this very moment, not the 'you' that you hope to be or plan to be or wish to be. No, it is the 'you' that you are now. That is God in action. Can you fathom that? Can you begin to feel the unconditional love surrounding the magnificent facet of creation that you are? You are the missing piece in all that you are searching. You are the God that you seek.

Come to the complete love and acceptance of all that you are, perceived warts and all. Love until you believe that you are quite done loving and you will find the love expand and your God Self with it.

We are with you always, goading you into the love of yourself for therein lies the key. Love yourself as you are in this very moment and in the most odious or desperate of moments for you are the God that you are, even in these moments. It is simply your judgement of yourself that separates you from that realization. In reality nothing can separate you from the God that you are.

This is the veil that so many speak of; it is a veil of judgement that you place upon yourself that creates the separation between what you believe to be God and yourself. All is God and God is one. Accept this truth into the depths of your being. Ask that it is done.

WE ARE YOUR BROTHERS IN ARMS

Who are you?

We are your brothers in arms. Your arms are the extension of our limbs, your heart is the extension of our heart and your mind is the tool we co-jointly use to make you function on Earth. We are a delicate and intricate machinery of functioning humanity; the extension and expression of your Spirit Self. We all fit into your physical expression. The physical expression is the cloak of our being. It is the vehicle through which we venture on this planet called Earth.

What is our purpose?

Our ultimate purpose together, is to come to the most complete expression of who we are within the confines of the physical expression here on Earth. Your physical expression is the funnel for our united being.

Why do you speak of yourselves in the plural?

The being that you are encompasses a multitude of definitions and characteristics intertwining constantly and revolutionarily. It is forever spiralling in evolution, metamorphosing without cease, ebbing and flowing, pulsating in a continual dance of renewal. We are this pulse, this heartbeat of universal life and God, which is `you`.

Imagine that you are one of a multitude of veins in your physical body, magnified in universal terms. You are part of the life force of `All That Is`. You are the constant pulse of life. You cannot die or degenerate. You are always part of this flux of life, and your experience here is but a vehicle that you have chosen for a specific trip. It is a mode of transport in a sea of experiences that feed the life force of `All That Is`. You are eternal and your eternity sojourns in the `you` that you experience concurrently. Let us all enjoy the trip.

THE HEART COMMAND

Start functioning through your heart. You have been trained to function through the mind, giving it dominance over everything. Your task now is to give dominance to your heart and your intuition.

Effective free will flows from this connection between the heart and the mind. It has been ruptured and requires reconnection so that you can remember `All That You Are`; your entirety. Become literally heart-centred and make your brain obey the command of the heart.

How do I know the heart command?

The command of the heart is a knowing that brings you to action with joy and certitude. It is a pulse of knowingness that makes you feel whole and desired. It is an impulse of love that is felt within your being which prevents you from doubting or fearing.

What happens if I do not obey the heart command?

If you do not obey the heart command you simply miss precious opportunities to express this fullness of you. You live less than in the totality that you are. You live just a little less. It is neither good nor bad it is simply just less than you are.

What are the consequences of living less than I am?

A consequence is a decrease in the joy quotient that you deserve and that you are. You diminish your lot of joy and freedom.

Is this accumulative?

It is most certainly accumulative but it is instantaneously reversible and available. Your joy is never lost and is reclaimable at any moment. You never ultimately lose out on your joy but you delay the opportunity to feel it. All is perfect in the universe and the time for you to reclaim your total and utter joy, that is you, is already here. It exists in parallel to you at all times. When you function from your linear mind, you cannot access it fully. Your heart centre is therefore the portal to this parallel universe and the key to its opening.

Tell me more please about accessing this heart space.

It is through the conscious breath. It is so simple that it bypasses the intellect. To practise the conscious breath requires humility and patience and ultimately love of the self. The conscious breath will allow you automatic access to this parallel universe.

Is it possible to consciously breathe all day long?

It is an almighty switch of beingness to consciously breathe because it makes you feel initially as if you are doing nothing of great use. To help convince your intellect into feeling that it is doing and achieving something consider that this breath is like a large key opening the door to this parallel universe.

This is the greatest training for learning to be, and allowing life to dance with you in great freedom and joy. In and through these moments of consciously breathing you become the bellows of all existence. Your beingness expands the world as you know it and allows you to escape the confines of your linear way of doing and existing.

Do not fear that you will become a being of nothingness and non-achievement. You will simply be a being, existing in the Universe in which you belong, unfettered and unhindered by the restraints of your bossy and somewhat unruly intellect masquerading as wisdom. Wisdom is a knowingness that originates in the mind of the heart. Awaken the mind of the heart and allow the little mind to obey its orders.

Why am I afraid to live in that parallel universe of joy and unfettered freedom? I feel like I sabotage myself continually as if it is all too much to bear.

The conditioning is stringent in its hold. This conditioning has been the leader of the pack for so long and resists being surpassed in any decisions. It requires a consistent and sustained effort on your part to dethrone it but the payoff is enormous in return, and the benefits to everyone in your vicinity accrue as you become more and more the example of how to live in this parallel universe of freedom and joy.

When I am finding it painful to consciously breathe because the emotion I am experiencing is so strong, what then?

Do what you can, and release all need for change. Be easy with yourself and love yourself exactly where you are, for all is ultimately and unconditionally perfect. Where you are right now is exactly where you need to be. By surrendering to the knowledge that you are exactly where you need to be, you come right back into the moment and into your beingness.

Judgement places you out of yourself and into a past or future scenario and so out of the `present` of the moment. To judge yourself in any way is to disown your heritage and your divinity. Do not even judge yourself for judging yourself; that is like a dog trying to catch its own tail. Let your tail wag whichever way it wants and be content with where you are now.

If where I am is too painful, then what do I do?

Accept totally that it feels really painful and know that this too will pass. Seek help and comfort from a beloved soul that knows what it is to feel this pain and who can give balm to your wounds with emotional and spiritual healing. Everything is ultimately an emotional wound and the emotion is there to be expressed. Emotion is a feeling in motion, when it gets stuck it creates pain so that it calls out for the attention it seeks. It is in receiving the emotion that we receive the gift of `present` time.

Much of the pain of the emotion comes from wanting the emotion to go away and so it expresses itself with greater force for it too seeks resolution and liberation. Its task ultimately is to bring you freedom and in doing so it earns its freedom. Therefore it is important to acknowledge it and allow it expression. Speak with it and breathe it through your body so that it can give you its messages and learning. The present is unwrapped when you fully embrace the emotion and feel it in the present moment; that magic place that allows you to access the parallel universe.

And this is precisely sometimes where you cheat yourself, for you judge the emotion thinking you are somehow weak to feel anger, sadness or despair and so you ignore the present that this emotion has come to give you. So much effort to avoid what is ultimately a present sitting unwrapped.

Why are we so afraid of emotion?

Your sense of emotion overwhelms you. You feel that it is much bigger and grander than it is and that ultimately it will consume you. It is the resistance of the emotion that is all consuming. There is nothing to fear once you have embraced the emotion. So welcome it and let it move through you with love. Honour the emotion with love and give it value for the messages it carries. Emotions are but passing messengers sent to bring you freedom and light. Do not leave the gift unopened by the doorstep.

So how do we fully receive the emotion?

You do so with the help of the conscious breath. Breathe these emotions that you resist into the very tips of your fingers and toes and watch what happens.

You make it sound so simple.

It is simple indeed, but not easy. With practice you will enter into this conscious exchange and it is through the conscious breath that the practice is enhanced and mastered.

What is so important about the heart space?

The heart space is the seat of the soul of `All That Is You`. It is the portal or access point to everything that you need to know and feel. When you experience love and assurance this is a sign that the portal has been accessed.

The breath is the key to this portal, and feelings of love and assurance act as a keypad.

Gratitude accesses the love and encourages the sentiment of assurance. `All is well`. Say this and feel your heart engage.

Is this the physical heart?

Within the heart space are cells of intelligence that read the mind of the heart. They relate this information to the rest of the physical vessel, sending messages to the physical realm and beyond.

Is this portal access to our Higher Being?

This is the highway.

What is the soul?

Your soul is the essence bearer of `All That Is You`.

Can the soul improve in this lifetime or does it contain the total magnitude of 'All That Is Me'?

It is without boundaries, without limitation, without definition, without plan or need for permission. It is.

I am beginning to see that my soul is held within my heart space. My heart space is eternal and spherical in form, and that my physical body is the golden casket for this heart space.

This heart space is the portal to my full being that is neither above nor below, nor behind, nor in front. It is simply the portal to the infinity of 'All That Is'.

This is a paradigm shift in representation for me as I have always imagined having to go up to my Higher Being or Office, up to my real self, residing in an imagined heaven above me.

Indeed, this is a good image. You, as in you, the human self, are a golden casket holder for 'All That You Are' which is limitless, formless in essence and of a magnitude unimaginable currently from where you reside. It is pliable to the will of you; that is this being here and now that you call 'you'.

Where does the will of me here and now reside?

There is an ongoing conflict between the will of the mind and the thrust of the heart-mind in the heart space we have just described. This is the battle we speak of.

Where do resolution and peace abide in the 'me' here?

Fully access the heart and the totality of existence is yours for the sharing, taking and absorbing. This is the mighty portal to 'All That You Are', concurrently and forever.

LAY DOWN YOUR WEAPONS

You have become very adept at hiding your light for fear that it will be spotted, and that you will be ridiculed for believing in such intangible things. This fear of ridicule, this fear of being 'discovered' has become part of your way of being in the world.

Now is the time for the paradigm shift within your being in the world. You do not have to become a street preacher or a preacher in any form, but you can now stop yourself from denigrating your being, from being less than who you are, from being smaller than your true grandeur.

We see you fitting into a new suit of armour, shiny and polished, not made from metal but instead tiny little golden rings. Each ring represents the eternity of you, gold because your life experiences have made it so, and numerous because the experiences have been multiple. Wear this armour with the pride of one that has fought a long and hard battle and has defeated the foe.

Tell the story of your success in battle. The foe has appeared inherently indefatigable but you have battled on, despite your weariness and your lassitude and your waning hope, to struggle onwards in this battlefield of love, fighting for the love of yourself despite everything seemingly robbing you of this love that is rightfully yours.

It is time to lay down your weapons and your defences and embrace the victory that you have won over yourself. You have not believed the lies that have told you that you are less than, or undeserving, or punishable, or incomplete. You have allowed the tiny light of your being to continue shining in the recess of your heart and it is this minuscule light that has brought redemption to your life. It has brought you back to the fullness of you, and now the adventure of love can really begin. Welcome back.

WHO ARE YOU TO YOURSELF?

To know a fact is to snatch it from rote, but to really understand it, is to have lived and experienced it. That is why you must traverse the sometimes inhospitable terrains of emotion. It is so that this understanding can become the compassion and empathy from which you can live and love your community.

And when we speak of community we mean the community of 'Who You Are' in the largest sense of the term. You are not just benefiting your fellow humans in your experiencing but that learning expands to beyond what you perceive in the physical realms.

The emotional experience is something you modulate and commune with and, ultimately, fashion. Imagine that you are completely assailed by an emotion and it is an unpleasant emotion like fear or depression or boredom or lassitude.

What does a sail do when it is assailed by the wind? If the sail is caught out of shape, facing in the wrong direction to the wind, it will flap violently making a terrible raucous, sending the boom in all directions eventually causing either harm to the helm or capsizing the boat completely. Some sailors like the taste of salt water but ultimately it becomes exhausting to have to haul yourself countless times out of the water back into the boat and continue your journey cold, tired, wet and miserable.

However, if a sail is in the hands of a good sailor, being assailed by the wind becomes a joyful challenge. The boat will move lightly and swiftly through the water and will make great speed giving the helm a thrill.

When the wind is too strong no wise sailor will venture out. So when the emotions are too assailing, take time just to be still. Let the whirl of the assailment move around you concentrically in spirals of dynamic moving emotion. Stay inside the boat club, inside the eye of the storm, inside with your innermost self, giving *yourself* comfort and love and safety.

When you are in the grasp of an emotion, do not try to figure it out. Move into a place of deliberate stillness and move to the core of the love that you are. Try not to search it from outside yourself but imagine this furnace of love just below where you imagine your heart to be. It is a stove of love designed to help you traverse the most difficult terrain. It is a hearth of love, comfort and nurture and reminds you that you are love, you are light, you are safety and you are beautiful, and out of any situation that you may find yourself in there are only the most loving of solutions to choose from. Just know that you are well. Give yourself the love that you seek. Give yourself the security that you yearn. Give yourself the abundance that you covet. Give yourself the time that you require to feel at peace within yourself.

There are many pathways, many therapies, many gadgets, many prophesies, many secrets told and untold but ultimately the core of the solution lies completely in your hands and in your heart and at the hearth of who you are to yourself.

Who are you to yourself?
Who are you to yourself?
Who are you to yourself?

YOU ARE INSEPARABLE FROM YOUR BROTHERS AND SISTERS

Your great fortune is to be walking this path consciously in awareness of the many energetic pulsations that are invading your living space daily. Even your human consciousness cannot fully comprehend the vast array of modifications to your being that are constantly happening; it would be too much for you to register or understand. It is not surprising therefore that you sometimes feel a little frazzled. This feeling of being frazzled is exacerbated by your difficulty to access your inner pillar of strength; your place of knowing in which the peace of your mind and heart can align. We would encourage you greatly to align these two centres of consciousness; your mind and your heart. You do not need any elaborate breathing or visualization techniques. Simply speak to each centre as if to two dear friends and request of them to align for the greatest good of all.

Everything you do or realize is done and realized for `All That Is`. You are inseparable from your brothers and sisters so when you are aligning yourself you are automatically helping your dear brothers and sisters to do likewise. Commune also with your brothers and sisters in nature; allow the trees to caress you with their branches and the grass to tickle the soles of your feet. You meld with `All That Is` by allowing nature to nurture you. Being in nature also calibrates your physical, emotional and mental bodies helping you to be more comfortably present. It awakens an inner strength that will be tangible to you.

Do not try to overcomplicate your being with particular techniques. To simply breathe and be thankful are very powerful modalities. Rest easy and know that, although sometimes you choose to feel alone, you are in fact surrounded by help and aid, comfort and nurturance. We are at your greatest service. Our love and respect for you are boundless dear ones.

THE UNIVERSE BENDS TO YOUR WILL

Whichever way you look at things is the way that they bend. The universe is so loving and compassionate that it will literally bend to your will. It will conform to the view which you impose upon it, for it wishes to reflect to you how you see yourself.

When you gaze upon something with awe then you see reflected the awareness of your majesty. When you limit your view to work and no play this is what shows up too. What you see of the world does not come from outside yourself it quite literally comes from within which is why, when you meditate, your expansiveness is revealed to you, and is then reflected back to you in your reality of the day.

So what happens when we see weakness, frustration and anger?

These are reflections that are likewise to be owned. As soon as you hear yourself saying, "she is such a cross person" or "he is so mean with his words", change the `he` or `she` to `I` and then with complete compassion for all that you are, accept that as your own. You are also these reflections. This is not so that you can find another stick with which to beat yourself but it is so that you can accept that all is part of you and you are part of the all.

It is in the recognition of this reality that you can come to terms with the completeness of yourself, and love yourself for all that you are; perceived warts and all. This will also teach you not to become frustrated and angry when somebody is hurtful towards you. This is your hurt and difficulty also, and when you accept it fully as also being yours then you alchemize the harm and become full onto yourself.

This is a constant practice. See all that comes to you as being part of you, not outside yourself at all, and bring it to you with open arms, whatever it may be, and you will find peace in yourself. As long as you hold it outside of yourself and place the blame on someone else you cause suffering to yourself and the other person.

This is a complete switch of thinking patterns. You are learning to communicate with everything that comes your way, not as something to be controlled or judged but something to be embraced fully, however it presents itself.

RELISH IT LIKE YOU DO YOUR CHOCOLATE

This itching to do, to perform and be celebrated for what you do, stems from an inner separation with source. For peace of mind, heart, soul and body, the constant communication, whether that be verbally, intellectually, emotionally, with that source of 'All That You Are', will sustain every single iota of your being. It will regulate all and everything. Be obedient to it alone, and become sufficiently still in yourself until it is your only guiding force. This requires discipline and dedication but the rewards are beyond what you can imagine.

Do not waste a moment of mistrust of yourself or the life that you are leading. Be at one with 'All That You Are'. Feel the deliciousness of the present moment and relish it like you do your chocolate. Everything is flowing from this source.

When you drink from a pure water source nothing else afterwards will taste as good. You have access to this pure spiritual source at all times, and it will literally dictate your next best step. So follow it, drink of it and enjoy.

SHOOT TO THE HEART OF THE MATTER

Know that you are strong and that you have a strength that is vaster, deeper, wider and more inexhaustible than you can imagine. Just know that this strength will take you everywhere, even calmly through death when you face it.

In the recognition of this strength there is no need to fear for you will always move forward and through any challenge that comes your way.

The secret is not to be critical of yourself in the process. Just keep acknowledging your strength. You have access to a strength that makes you highly effective. Trust in your strength and your beauty of spirit. Trust that all is well and constantly unfolding for the good of all.

Strength of love and purpose are indefatigable and hit the mark every time. Pick up the bow and arrow and shoot to the heart of the matter.

A DIP IN THE OCEAN

Regard your sojourn here as a dip in the ocean. There are many creatures in the ocean sharing the same milieu, the same surroundings, the same source of life, and yet each one has a singular task with regard to the overall functioning of the ecosystem. Each entity expresses itself in a completely different form, whether that is at a microscopic or gigantic level of creative expression. There are constant dynamics that are altering the reality of these creatures and yet each is surrounded and bathed by the same reality; the ocean.

And so it is for you human beings. You are in it all together, this same bath of reality, and likewise each of you has a singular task of beingness that defines you. This definition of who you are sends out a singular vibratory form that is registered as an integral part of this bath of reality.

And so as you grow to express more of who you are at a divine level the bath of reality shifts to accommodate this new expansion, and as a result the bath of reality is forever modified for all that swim in it. Every expression of life in the bath of reality is exposed, through osmosis, to this new modification to the bath of reality, and as such has the opportunity to expand likewise.

There are parts of the ocean that are so deep that darkness reigns everywhere. The creatures that navigate in these depths are suited to living in darkness. Their bodies have adapted to living without light and they know no different. And yes indeed, as you have guessed, the same happens in the human realms. Imagine the adaptation that is required to becoming accustomed to living with more light. Everything in the psyche and physical realms needs to learn to adapt to living with more light, and so the process of awakening or enlightenment is often slow for these reasons.

Darkness is a state without light and so is finite. Lightness is exponential, it is forever brighter and greater and more luminous; it is an eternal and exquisite and never-ending discovery. Do not be impatient for the journey to end for there is no end.

We wish for you to accept all manner of life expressions without judgement or division. All of life adapts to where it finds itself and for many this is simply a question of trying to survive in the dark.

Be grateful for all and everything. Be not in judgement but follow the torch of light that you are graced with and shine your torch because the beams of light stretch far and wide beyond your scope and reach.

Imagine that you are that torch and from your heart shines the light. Charge the torch with your intention and your love and let it shine light where there is darkness. Allow your heart to be in control of the torch, as the mind will want to switch off the light. Notice that the light shines without noise or fanfare. It just is, and as it shines outwards from the torch the beam becomes wider and wider. Let it be so.

We stand holding the torch at the portal of your heart.

THE REALM OF MAKE-BELIEVE

The only relationship of importance is the relationship you have to and with yourself. Everything else, without exception, is a reflection of that relationship; lack, poverty, war, anger, joy, resilience, ecstasy, jealousy, reluctance, enthusiasm, wickedness, chaos, discipline, waywardness, lust, passion, melancholy, desire, despair, abundance. Every moment of every emotion is a reflection of your relationship with yourself.

It is for this reason that you feel emotion, as the emotion is the barometer of where you are in that relationship. What feels constricted and sad and unpleasant is simply the red light signal for a rupture of communication with the 'All That Is'. Flashing, warning, please come back into alignment with 'All That You Are', so that you can feel the joy, fulfilment, abundance and delight of the great being that you are.

These emotions are acting as friend not foe, and part of the difficulty in being human is that you have judged these barometer emotions as being something that you cannot and do not want to experience. You treat them as the foe when they arise and you do battle with them rather than welcoming them as a friend that has a tale to tell or a gift to impart.

When emotions that you do not enjoy arise, greet them as a friend, ask them to tell their tale, accept their gift and then let them be on their way. Each emotion will have a truly beautiful tale to tell if you allow it to. It is a passing guest though. It will stay only for as long as it is useful to you; just a short visit, long enough to impart its news.

When you manage to do this systematically with all the unpleasant emotions that arise for you in a day then you will be communing with your GPS system. This is your fail-safe system which will permit you to see where you fall out of love with yourself.

MAY THY WILL BE DONE ON EARTH AS IT IS IN HEAVEN

Every grain of sand in the desert has been honed from the whole; one almighty piece of stone or rock, at some stage. Can you imagine such a scale of creation; that from the whole came the many pieces that in their gazillions create a desert?

Each sphere of being, as in the human being, is like a grain of sand in the whole desert, each one honed from the rock of creation so that it could again redefine itself.

How could you deny the full expression of any of the individual grains of sand? You cannot. And so it is neither for you to judge nor condemn but to simply allow each grain of sand to express itself in its fullness, whatever that expression may be.

Each grain of sand will be exposed to the same elements; the sand storms, further erosion, displacement, extremes of temperature, and for each grain of sand the experience will be distinct and individualized. No two grains of sand will experience the desert in the same way.

Every experience you have therefore is of universal benefit to the rock of creation. None of it is forbidden or judged, for how can the rock of creation deny any part of itself no matter how minuscule it may look or feel?

You are seeing now that this realm, this earthly experience, is sacred in its offering of experience to you. Cherish each experience as the passageway to the recreation of 'All That You Are'. Bring every grain of sand into your being so that you can feel the strength, solidity and wholeness of the rock of creation that you are.

All is truly well in this world. You cannot be involved in any experience that is not ultimately for your wellbeing. All is well and unfolding as it can and should and may. Be at peace always dear hearts. Lean on us, we urge you.

IT IS A MATTER OF THE HEART

The only effective form of functioning in and of the world is through the heart space. The heart space opens you to a new form of language, a new code of conduct, a new reality. To access this heart space you must be very vigilant, for the mind would have you think that it is the master.

To master one's life means mastering your living through the heart space. From this space everything takes on a new significance, a new vibration, a different hue, another perfume, an eternal joyfulness and happiness, an inherent easiness and deliciousness that will leave you fully satiated.

Just imagine that your breath flows in and out through your heart. Imagine at your heart, pink petals tinged with white. Watch the flower of your heart open and close rhythmically to the sound of your tune; the rhythm of your breath.

Keep putting one foot in front of the other with as much courage and love as you can muster. Keep loving all that you do, all that you are and all who you are with.

Love, laugh, dance and sing.

MAY I BE THE LOVE, I WISH TO ENJOY

You are moving into a time in which communication is being recognized as the valuable tool that it is. Solutions are presenting themselves which, more and more, involve the co-creation of both parties, even if one of the parties is deemed to have more authority. This is an important and mature development in the psyche of humanity and it is one that, gradually but surely, is leading to a progressive enlightenment process. You are realizing that it is incumbent upon you to find solutions that benefit both parties. You are beginning to see in your daily dealings that this is necessary for the peace and happiness of all involved.

This is the loving of others as you love yourself. This is kindness in action for it is saying, "Your wellbeing is as important as my wellbeing". It is asking the question, "What can we do so that both of us enjoy the happiness and contentment that we both deserve?"

This is an extremely powerful paradigm for it literally turbo boosts the universal level of happiness available to all. If, in all of your dealings, you were able to adopt this simple principle of being: that my happiness is yours and yours is mine, then you would act differently and begin to experience life differently.

Say to yourself:
May I be the love, I wish to enjoy.
May I be the joy, I wish to share.
May I be the compassion, I wish to receive.
May I be the freedom, I wish to experience.

Peace to your heart, to your mind, to your soul, to your longings and your desires. Peace to the very core of your being in which the love of your self is pure and true and unadulterated. Be still for this moment, and the next, knowing that all is well.

EVERY BREATH IS A GIFT

This human existence is a beautiful and exquisite journey in coming back to the full realization of 'All That You Are'.

Know that your every breath is a gift from the Creator. If you were to live knowing that every breath is a gift, what would you do with this breath? Would you squander it? Would you take it for granted? Would you embrace it fully acknowledging the gift of life that courses your being? What makes that next breath come? Try withholding your breath indefinitely. You cannot.

Life wants to illuminate your soul and, in doing so, it breathes life into you.

Life wants to express its beauty through you and, in doing so, paints the picture that you are.

Life wants to experience itself and, in doing so, brings this picture of you to life so that it can feel and touch and be.

Life wants its creations to learn from one another, grow with one another, expand with one another and so it creates the brotherhood and sisterhood that humanity is.

You are part of this desire for life to live, love and laugh. Without your full participation there will be a part of life not completely lived. Embrace life with the faith and trust of your childlike self. Fall into her lap like you would fall into the lap of a loving mother knowing, that even if you fall, she will pick you up and cuddle you and fix your scraped knee.

Life wants to be lived by you. Will you allow it? Your breath is the invitation and your response. Breathe deeply and consciously, in gratefulness for this invitation, to be the full expression of life being lived.

BE THE METEOROLOGIST OF YOUR MIND

When you are running alongside the sea something changes deep within your being. You become the mirror to the image that the sea is giving. The sea is like your thoughts. When it is calm you feel calm and uplifted and at ease in yourself. When it is windy and choppy you have to exert yourself to push through the wind and you may feel dishevelled and blown about or perhaps more enlivened than usual.

And so it is with your thoughts. When you look at yourself in the mirror you are seeing the sea of thoughts that infiltrate your mind. You are not beholding the definitive image of you for that image is forever adapting to the sea of thoughts that wave upon your mind. And for you to pick upon a detail within this sea with the desire to change it is as futile as wanting to stop the waves upon the shore.

You should instead govern the conditions that govern the sea. And so become the meteorologist of your mind. Bring in the sunshine, introduce a fresh invigorating breeze, blow away the clouds and call in the tuneful melodies of the birds of the sky.

Make the situation ideal in your head and what you see in the sea of life will change before your very eyes.

YOU WIN SOME, YOU LOSE SOME

You never lose at anything you do in life for losing is winning. When you lose you are actually gaining or winning in clarity and focus, as your intentions and your real desires gain a laser focus. When you win, you are sometimes losing something else whether that is time to yourself or gaining attention you do not seek.

The real winning and losing is a game played out in your mind. If you can know, in that deep place within, that you are forever a winner then everything must align with this belief.

MOMENTS OF STASIS

Often when the doubts arise it is as if a blizzard descends blocking the view all around. In these moments of `whiting-out`, it is the call for you to be at one with the situation at hand. It is a calling to be at peace with all that you see your life to be, as it is, without trying to change it, modify it, review it or preview it. The blizzard closes in so that all that you can see is within. This is a precious gift. You do not like it because it causes a feeling of panic; a feeling of stasis. It challenges the status quo which is one of doing, action, moving forward.

Get comfortable with these moments of stasis because they are the moments in which the connection between head and heart is being established. Imagine the following scene: a few lanes have been blocked along the motorway and traffic is moving slower. The repair and upgrade work means however that soon you will have a motorway with four lanes on each side rather than two, so that the traffic can flow smoothly again without delay.

So do not beat up on yourself when you feel yourself slowing down, this is the heavenly upgrading service in full swing. All too soon you will be at your destination.

And where is that destination? It is heartland, homeland, back at the hearth of your home, nestled within `All That You Are`.

GO WITH THE FLOW

You are in an ever continuing circle of renewal and re-blossoming, and each and every time your blossoms will reveal a different and hitherto unseen colour. No two rejuvenations or periods of re-blossoming are identical. You are therefore forever evolving. You do not feel that you change but you are changing incessantly.

And so be aware that this is likewise the case for others around you. To place judgement on yourself or another is misplaced because the judgement, as soon as it is made, is no longer valid as a change has already come in the interim. In fact, your judgement is relevant to an observation of the past and not ever of the present.

The present, therefore, is a constant present, in that it is a constant new discovery and gift to you. Your Universe is so tight a tapestry of interwoven experiences, discoveries and renewals that you cannot fathom even the tiniest percentage of such intricacy. That is why it often presents as the 'same old thing' but never is it. So accept the spirals of further and complete evolution that are occurring at all times and know that you are intricately a part of this spiralling evolution.

Go with the flow on all things because your belief that you can change or modify anything penetrates only the tiniest part of the vast intricacy of life. Instead allow yourself to be carried on the universal wave and flow of life; the multi-patterned majesty of creation, recreation and rejuvenation.

THE PATH OF CREATION

You are constantly on the path of creation, of realization, of growth and of learning. However in those moments, which feel like stasis, your growth is actually reaching a particular apogee. In these moments you are required to be still without much external interference because internally you are all of a whirl, whether you are consciously aware of that or not.

We are at a time again of upheaval and whirling changes of movement within the human psyche because you are letting go of hitherto held beliefs. When you hold a belief it is like exercising a muscle in isolation; it becomes exhausting and painful. Sometimes the shock treatment is required to let you go of a belief system that does not serve your growth or indeed your present circumstances.

Let us give you an image: a man goes to his shed in the garage and pulls out the lawnmower ready to cut his new lawn. He knows that he cannot cut it too short as the roots are shallow and so he cuts at the lowest height possible for the lawnmower. As he cuts he realizes that even this shallow depth is too much and the lawnmower is actually tearing the freshly grown grass out of the soil. He has to stop quickly so that the rest of the lawn is not damaged and, by doing so, he saves his lawn and its future growth.

And it is the same with your spiritual growth. If you start pulling at fresh seeds of knowledge before they have the time to bed down in your consciousness you affect your overall wellbeing. The grass will only grow back in those places where the grass has been reseeded and has had time to root in the soil. And so your old and outdated belief systems leave an unsown space that must be reseeded with beliefs that suit your further spiritual growth, wonderment, knowledge and wellbeing.

Once the grass seedlings have penetrated deep enough into the soil then the lawnmower can pass over them and the grass will grow again even more lusciously than before with more vigour. Once you have the opportunity to integrate the new learning you can also test it and play with it so that it can grow lusciously within you.

So to tend fully to yourself, honour these times of introspection as the seedlings of new belief and vision burrow deep within the soil of your soul. Once embedded these new seedlings of belief will grow strong but at the beginning tend to those seedlings of new belief with care, watering them without testing them too heavily. All is well.

WHO AM I, AND WHAT AM I DOING HERE?

"Who are you not?" is more the question. You spend more time *not* being 'All That You Are' than 'All That You Are' but that is a result of the modus operandi of your time and space. To be 'All That You Are' you have to dream and be of the dream. You have to allow your thoughts to fly high.

Do daydream. Bring yourself to that feeling place that says, "I feel good, I feel whole, I feel complete, I feel inspired and at ease. All is well in my life. All is well", and linger there for as long as you can. Linger there in full cognizance of the beauty and ease of 'All That You Are'. That is the real secret: finding ease where easily you could talk yourself out of it.

When you are asked to go with the flow it means that you must stop the sabotaging, in your mind, of that sense of ease with yourself, your circumstances, your space, your time, your situation; your perpetual habit of finding fault or imperfection.

Try as incessantly to be at ease, as incessantly as you try not to be, and watch what happens. All that you desire to be will come flowing to you because you are not talking yourself out of it.

All that you desire wants to flow to you but it takes one look at you as you are shaking your head or being down on yourself, or feeling unloved and looking sad, and all that you desire just knows that you will not recognize it when it gets to you. It waits for the moment when it can be bountifully and wholly recognized for 'All That *It* is', as it so loves itself that it cannot exist in the unloved state.

So, in essence, your task is easy. Be at ease with all that you are and that includes all of your creations. Be at ease with exactly who and what you perceive you have become. Chill about it all and watch the bounty seek you out.

All is well.

OVERINDULGENCE

Overindulgence is not possible so it is not something that you should fear. It is the fear of overindulging that creates the need to do it. Somewhere in your psyche you are convincing yourself of lack, or deprivation, or of the need for self-punishment; in short it is the result of lack of love. This lack of love is not punishable either for it just is a pattern of behaviour learned from a miscoded series of belief systems.

What causes damage is this incessant hate of yourself, and the continual feeling that you have to improve yourself. To find balance it is necessary to fall in love with all aspects of yourself; everything about you. If that is too difficult to do, just start by not beating up on yourself. Do not allow yourself to be unkind to yourself, and then get out and about and do lots of walking and hiking and enjoying yourself outdoors.

Do what you love. What makes you think that being inside is what you love?

You could walk everywhere and love it.

Do that, start walking everywhere and love it.

NO NEED FOR VALIDATION OF WHO YOU ARE

We would like you to know that all is well and that everything is working out for your greatest good and that you do not need to validate who you are anywhere else than in your own heart of hearts.

You already have a direct connection to source through your own heart portal as it streams simultaneously in and out, threading through your desires and almost-manifestations into a reality that you can then recognize and dance with.

IMPERVIOUSNESS

Imperviousness to the so-called realities of life allows you to stay in the stillness zone. Whatever appears is but a whirlwind of activity and reaction; a chemical reaction to elements combining. When you stay in the zone of stillness then these reactions are simply a fireworks display; an outplaying of the chemical reactions of your imaginings. Watch them as if you are watching a spectacle. Do not become involved, because in doing so you add elements to the reaction that may ignite it further.

Stay still within. Stay impervious to the reactions, but not to the source of 'All That Is' which is the stillness you are seeking. From this stillness comes action but action that is led from one element; the element of love which has a wide bandwidth of vibration and consumes all that it is not.

Love consumes all that it is not, just as light dispels the darkness. Love is all there is. Love is the only element required in the combustion of reality. Make love the only element that you test tube. Allow it to overflow, to heal and bring into its reaction all the other elements that would seek to explode or combust in unpleasant ways.

When an event has upset you imagine placing it in a flame of love. Imagine this flame to be blue with an orange centre. Watch as you trim the flame and then hold above it a test tube containing all the reactions or dramas that you have encountered that day. As the test tube is heated by the flame, the dramas of the day are transformed into a violet flame of love and all is well. Believe this to be true, and so it is.

THE FUTURE VERSUS THE PRESENT

It is of less importance what you wish to do or achieve in the future, as that is in a future place. What is much more crucial is: what is it that you are presently thinking or doing? Where is your attention in this moment?

You can feel yourself resisting wanting to do this. That is that survival part of your being that is looking out for you, trying to keep you in the 'doing' mode, so that you will always do what is necessary to keep you safe. That is a valid and necessary part of your being but it can mislead you and does so regularly. It will speak of lack and will convince you that you do not know enough or are not good enough or that you do not earn enough. There will always be an underlining sense of lack; that is how, in fact, you will recognize that side of your being.

When you recognize it, thank it for being so thoughtful as to want to take all your concerns to its awareness, but instruct it not to worry any more as you have everything under control, and in that same moment simply ask your Higher Office to note the concern and deal with it.

Then you can live without worry and allow inspiration to be your guide, and all action or doing will arise from that place of inspiration. Practice this religiously and watch what happens.

THE ROLE OF THE HEART

Your car would not advance without an engine nor can your physical being function without an engine of propulsion. Obviously therefore, in physical terms, your heart is indispensable.

This indispensability however is relevant in equal measure to your sense of wellbeing as the heart is an accurate barometer of your faith in life and your faith in yourself. Your faith in yourself is directly related to your faith in life, and at the moment of your birth you entered into a realm in which this faith in yourself and your environment was immediately put into question. It may have been within the first few seconds of birth when a well-meaning nurse or doctor questioned your height, your weight, your ability to breathe, your ability to respond. The effect of this questioning was felt immediately even in the most loving of environments.

With this questioning of your invincibility, in the form of judgement from outside yourself, was born the need to survive beyond and outside the confines of perfect imperviousness. This was the moment when the seed of doubt was sown. You agreed to be born into this doubt so that you could embrace it and move towards your natural state which is complete acceptance and alignment with exactly who and what you are at any given moment. That is why, in this moment of the introduction of doubt, your heart retained the infallible awareness and appreciation of your grandeur and your completeness.

While the umbilical cord was being removed from your navel, a struggle for survival was being awakened, and simultaneously an invisible umbilical cord or connection to your wholeness, your completeness, your all consuming wellbeing, was being solidified through the portal or entry point of your heart.

It is for this reason that you know that things are essentially alright when you relax and come back to that simple love of yourself. Place your hand on your heart and feel the inner connection to 'All That You Are'. Even if you cannot or do not wish to feel it, just acknowledge that it is there. It is your umbilical cord nourishment.

You knew that you would have to eventually search for your physical nourishment in this world once the umbilical cord connection to your mother was severed. At the disappearance of this physical umbilical cord the brain fired into survival mode, and you sometimes allow this survival mode to dominate so much that you forget the heart connection that is there to protect you, completely and utterly, under all conditions.

Bring hope back into your heart. Maintain faith that your heart can guide you in all situations and under all conditions. Your heart has all the recipes you require for your own happiness and contentment.

Renew your commitment to this soul connector. Simply place your hand on your heart and ask for it to be so. And imagine, in that moment of placing your hand upon your heart, that a doorway is opened through which all struggle will disappear, and sustenance, faith, hope and love will manifest.

YOU ARE FOREVER

There is an endless cycle of beginnings and endings; this is what the nature of life is. Look at your seasons as they dance from life to death and rebirth. Be in acceptance of these rhythms, as they are but rhythms in an endless form of spiralling creation. There is, in fact, no real ending, it just appears like that.

In winter nature lies dormant and, to the outside view, it would appear that all is dead but within this state of dormancy is the potential for regrowth and new life.

It is the same when your body leaves this Earth. It goes into a state of budding dormancy; a state of potential renewal. It goes to a place unseen so that in time a new rebirth, a new life can be born. So do not despair when a life is extinguished here on Earth; it is simply a process of rebirth.

You, the eternal Spirit, the bulb of the plant, are forever. You are forever spiralling in life. Your path is forever extending before you. Find your peace and your sense of rest in that knowledge here and now, and know that there is perfection to all timing. Relax in the knowledge of the perfection of time and trust it explicitly. All is well.

YOU HAVE NOTHING TO FEAR

If only you knew that there is nothing to fear because every experience, no matter what its hue, will bring you to a fuller expression of who you are. So you have nothing to fear other than the fear of fear itself.

When the fear arises embrace it with the power of your light. Shine upon it with your love and acceptance and in that very moment it shall dissolve.

When a worry arises, embrace it and bring it home into the expansiveness of your love, and surrender it to 'All That You Are'. Nothing is insurmountable for it is simply a question of bringing it to that place of love that is forever residing in you.

All is well. Make this your inner mantra. All is well in this very moment of time.

ABUNDANCE AND EASE

For abundance and ease simply open the space for receiving. When you are in earning or wanting mode you are sending the energy in an unhelpful direction. You are sending it outward in enquiry and need.

Reverse the direction of your enquiry and imagine a huge arrow, golden in hue, flowing directly from the universe in and through your crown chakra, a smaller green arrow directly into your heart, an orange arrow flowing into your solar plexus and a red arrow flowing into your base chakra. Activate these arrows individually or simultaneously whenever you feel the need, and imagine and know the abundance of the universe flow through these arrowed channels and into your body, moving through your spiritual and physical bodies and, from there, into manifestation.

From this natural abundant flow, activity will be initiated but it will flow from a place of already established abundance and not the energy of lack which cannot emulate the heights of abundance.

By calling on and graciously receiving goodness into your life, you are creating a circular form of life-giving energy so that the difference between giving and receiving will become almost imperceptible and shall meld into one complete circle. You will be of the flow and in the flow and abundance will be the driving dynamic of this circular and spiralling motion in life that will bring you to fulfilment and joy.

THE INDIGO LIGHT

The indigo light possesses a density of hue that moves through the physical with a speed and potency that is heightened in comparison to other hues.

Each colour carries with it a certain vibration and, as such, has a certain task. The indigo vibration cuts through illusion, sloth, hubris and lethargy. It explodes the density of this energy into white light and, as a result, dissipates what is stuck and inert. When you are feeling as if your record keeps playing in the same groove, use this indigo light. Imagine it moving down through your crown chakra to the heart chakra where it will radiate outwards in all directions spherically from your heart liberating you from this feeling of being stuck or unsure of how to move forward.

BEING ALONE

When it comes to being alone you must see the word `one` in it. It is the all coming to one, all one. So to be alone with yourself is the opportunity to become all with your oneness, to come into perfect harmony with your full being.

Look for opportunities to enjoy this moment of being fully and completely content in your own company. Look for ways to pass time in your own company getting to know yourself, learning to nurture yourself, finding out what gives you pleasure and joy in life.

You are taught, from an early age, to be at ease in your outgoing ways with others, which is important, crucial even to your wellbeing, but you are not taught how to go about being completely at ease with going inward, with being at ease with yourself and your emotions and your desires and your fears.

Being `all at one` with yourself, `alone`, is a powerful and majestic potential for happiness. Try it!

EVERYTHING IS OF RELEVANCE

Time is a precious commodity. To move effortlessly with it allows it to move with you and transport you to your desired outcome, just like a river flows to the mouth of the sea or ocean.

The journey along all parts of this river is of importance in that, like the river, you will pick up so much. Many facets of the experiences will become like a residue of rocks and silt that you will carry along with you all the way to the mouth of the river. What is significant about arriving at the mouth of the river is that your personal experience, along the flow of this individual river from its source to the mouth, melds into the larger experience of humanity which is represented by the sea or vast ocean.

Your individual experience pours into the vast expanse of communion or coming into union with the rest of humanity. All that you live matters because it all flows into the greater body of water; the vast ocean of experiencing the 'All That Is'.

BOTH SIDES OF THE EXPERIENCE

The interplay of opposites brings completion to an experience. The experience of opposites creates a circle to the experience in which you, as a human being, get to discover the full scope of intricacies. To experience one side of the duality would leave you with half the experience.

Half of the moon is regularly hidden to you and yet you know the other side is there. This hidden face of the moon will turn to face you at some stage again.

You are simply witnessing all the facets of creation when you are experiencing duality in your life. You are getting the opportunity to be face to face with 'All That Is'.

How else can you come to fully love and embrace all parts of yourself?

WHY IS THERE SO MUCH DESTRUCTION IN THE WORLD?

It is the cycle of birth, death and rebirth. Sometimes it is necessary that the acting out of the death process be obvious so that the new birth can be initiated. If the death and suffering were not so obvious the impetus to move in the dynamic flow of creativity and renewal would not be so acute or driven. In many ways your impetus is driven by its opposite.

So you are all serving one another in the constant dynamic and spiralling flow of creation. To be the God that you truly are, you must create anew and anew.

WE ARE ALWAYS AT YOUR SERVICE

Who am I really and truly?

To ask this question in such a helpless manner is an excuse on your part to ignore that, in this very moment, you are really perfect, true, impeccable and faultless as you are. This is how infinity sees you, for you are but an expression, through the medium of infinity, of presence. You are akin to a centre of data for infinity to see how it can realize itself fully. You are the experience! You are the river! You are the ocean!

So why must we suffer?

The suffering is an agreement with 'All that You Are'. It is the opportunity to experience the redemptive power of divine love, forgiveness, compassion and completeness. It is an opportunity to remove oneself from wholeness so that one can rediscover the wholeness in a fresh, new way. It is the opportunity to serve the whole, as one's suffering can alleviate the pain of another.

How does that work?

All experience is registered in the database of infinity for all time. To *consciously* experience suffering is an extraordinary gift in time, to all of life. It is the conscious realization of the experience in full that allows for the redemptive action of divine love to pour through, for such courage on the part of that soul must be rewarded. This is not to say that we encourage you to seek suffering but should it come to your door then your interaction with it can activate the redemptive power of love in majestic form which will, in turn, be used for the good of all.

It all seems like an elaborate Machiavellian plan that I am now somewhat unwillingly part of.

You tease us for you know that were your heart always full of the divine love nectar then you would know nothing else and so would have nothing with which to measure the fullness of your cup. This is what you desired again to know and experience; this imagined lack of love.

Now, through your learning, you know that you are forever connected to this infinite well of divine love and yet you still experience lack. Who is at fault here?

Now you are teasing me because I find I am incapable of connecting to this infinite well at all times and that really frustrates me.

Make a decision to access this well of love as consciously as you can in every moment you can arrest from your day and night. Try this really sincerely and faithfully from now and see what happens.

Will you help?

We are always at your service but we can only do your bidding so you must consciously ask us to be there in the moments when you struggle otherwise we are powerless to act on your behalf. Know that we have only your most favourable outcomes at heart but we too feel powerless when you choose to live unconsciously, and frankly you forget us very easily and quickly, and then come crying when you feel disconnected. This is not intended as a judgement but as an observation from those that love and adore you.

Ok, I`m with you. Let`s try. I shall come back to report! But before I do that please explain, what is divine love and how do I access it and recognize it?

DIVINE LOVE

You come to divine love when you accept that you are doing the best that you can at any moment in time. You feel it when you give yourself the present of acceptance. It shows up when you relish all that surrounds you, whatever form that takes. You are conscious of it when you stop struggling and begin trusting.

Divine love is not something you do. It is present always. It is what you do to yourself that makes you feel separate from it:

You punish yourself in your thoughts.

You think worrisome thoughts of lack and poverty.

You criticize others in your head.

You imagine what others are thinking of you. (This is strictly none of your business!)

You imagine somehow that you have to merit the love of the Almighty.

You imagine that you are not really doing your best.

You imagine that you missed a turn somewhere and actually should be living a completely different life somewhere else.

You imagine that God the Almighty has sent you here to test you and will ultimately find you lacking.

You imagine traps everywhere.

You imagine that wholeness, enlightenment, self-actualization, the full conscious states are something to be attained, to be striven for, to be merited through the action of grace administered by some benevolent God that will decide at some future moment that you are finally worthy.

In Heaven's Name have you not been told time and time again that you are all part and parcel of the infinite plan?

You are meant to live joyfully and blissfully. You are joy and bliss. Do not allow the various coats of limited self-belief, that you have donned, hide this truth from you one moment longer. We know that it is not easy but it is simple and with our help you can undo the knots that stop your flow. Let us help. We do not even ask you to do it. We ask you to ask us for help.

BE EASY WITH YOURSELF

Busyness is a replacement for a lack of real desire. Your desires must come from deep within and be respected greatly for the value of their origin.

Be easy at all times with yourself. You are already where you need to be.

A sense of achievement is found in every breath.

It is not what you do but who you are to yourself that is, in any moment, important.

Be at peace.

BE THE GOD THAT YOU WISH TO BEHOLD

Take ownership of the creative power of the God source that flows through your being, and allow it to flow into this blessed life. And as you give, you shall receive, and as you receive you shall desire to give, and the God, that we all are, will flow in ever expanding circles of creation and joy and delight.

Be the God that you wish to behold.

Do not wait for goodness to come and change the world. Be the goodness you wish to see in the world.

Have you that level of courage and commitment to yourself?

Can you be that kind, loving, sweet and encouraging to yourself?

Let us start there.

God is love in creation.

Be that love in creation. Transform all that you behold with the eyes of love.

What a delicious journey this is. Let us continue to travel together.

About the Author

From my early twenties I had been asking for and receiving personal messages of love, reassurance and wisdom in written form from, what I was invited to call, my 'Higher Office'.

The messages became so allegoric and transformational in nature that I decided to commit to receiving one message a day for a year. That year became four and the resulting communication is part one of 'The Treasure Is Within'.

Six months after completing part one and, what I believed at the time would be 'The Treasure Is Within' in its entirety, our youngest son was diagnosed with brain cancer. In the introduction I tell the story of how, because of our son's diagnosis and subsequent treatment, I lost faith in life, myself, God and my Higher Office, only to rediscover this faith in a completely new way by coming to truly understand the messages I had received.

Part two of 'The Treasure Is Within' is the continuation, post-diagnosis, of this communication and teaching with my Higher Office throughout a long and difficult but ultimately liberating 'rebooting' process that has helped me thankfully navigate the last seven years, and relish the present.

Lightning Source UK Ltd.
Milton Keynes UK
UKOW02f1538221116
288237UK00001B/59/P